The
Best Four
Years

ALSO BY ADAM SHEPARD

Scratch Beginnings

The Best Four Years

How to Survive and Thrive in College (and Life)

Adam Shepard

HARPER

NEW YORK • LONDON • TORONTO • SYDNEY

HARPER

HarperCollins books may be purchased for educational, business, or sales promotional use. For information please write: Special Markets Department, HarperCollins Publishers, 10 East 53rd Street, New York, NY 10022.

FIRST EDITION

Library of Congress Cataloging-in-Publication Data is available upon request.

ISBN 978-0-06-198392-4

13 14 15 OV/RRD 10 9 8 7 6 5 4 3

For you, the college student.
Cheers! To the best four (or five or six) years of your life.

Acknowledgments

Frankly, I don't have a long list of people that I need to thank for their assistance in the writing of this book. Sometimes, less is more, and my small team of editors did an *awesome* job working with this project. For their effort, my gratitude goes out to the following:

Zack Wynne, who has made the most of his college experience—and his life—despite not starting out as the "cool kid."

My pops, George Shepard, who gave me a laugh or two about how it "used to be" as we were working through the manuscript together.

My ma, Joanie Shepard, who always has creative ideas to add.

Scott Mckaig, who will do pretty much anything for a hundred dollars and a beer. His editing was the best hundred dollars I ever spent.

Molly Beam, who found time in her busy professional life to offer all kinds of input.

Courtney Wheeler, a real writer with a fancy degree in English, who kept me grounded with her red pen.

Sarah Rossini, who has made the most of several experiences in higher education, and who tore up my writing and ideas from beginning to end. She probably deserves an author credit.

My bro, Erik Shepard, a current college student, who has helped guide me and mentor me throughout my life. I'm always learning from you.

Serena Jones, who labored to clean up my often-careless writing. Thank you for your help, word to word, with the editing of this book.

My agent, Dan Strone, who carves time out of doing big deals to allow for the little guy to be published, as well.

And, perhaps most important, my editor, Michael Signorelli, who polished up a final draft that I can be proud of.

Contents

Contents

Introduction

In the dead of the night on a Wednesday evening in September, my pops and I hopped in his not-quite-ancient-but-acting-like-it '95 Ford Escort hatchback and strolled (and if you saw him drive, you'd know I mean strolled) our way up Interstate 95 on our way from Raleigh, North Carolina, to Andover, Massachusetts. There, I was to get situated for a weekend of orientation at Merrimack College before the best four-year run of my life would begin. It wasn't a straight shot up I-95 by any means, especially with old George finding "shortcuts" around major arteries that were almost certainly congested with traffic. "See all those folks?" he'd ask. "Those suckers don't know what they're getting into." He then bore right onto some auxiliary highway, where we'd avoid an hour jam in D.C. by going ninety minutes out of our way. "See that," he'd say. "Not a lick of traffic." He'd smile as if he was onto something potentially life changing. And I'd wonder where in the *hell* we were and if I was *ever* going to get to Merrimack.

But I didn't care. Somehow, I managed to sleep almost the whole way, despite my having agreed to spend half the trip driving. I'm certain Pops preferred it that way, though. My propensity to grind the gears of his stick shift had cost him one new clutch during my high school years, and he surely didn't want to make it two. We made the trip in sixteen hours. Four years later, my brother and I did it in eleven.

We stopped just shy of Massachusetts to get a hotel room and rest up for a busy day of unpacking the ridiculous amount of stuff I had packed. I'm talking about absolutely nugatory crap. (If you haven't already made this mistake, you will, despite my forewarning.) But the unpacking wasn't to be. At least not by our hands, anyway. We arrived on campus and followed the signs to my assigned residence hall, at which point our car was attacked by hordes of upperclassmen volunteers, who for whatever reason, had decided to come back to school three days early to aid the new kids with the challenging task of emptying the hundreds of useless articles out of our cars and into our new living quarters.

Then came forty-eight hours of orientation sessions and an evening of relaxation before school started on Monday. And boy, was I ill prepared for what was to come.

There are many reasons why I've chosen to write this book for you.

First, I'm giving you the opportunity to build your vocabulary beyond your wildest imagination with some of the three- and even four-syllable words I'm going to include throughout *The Best Four Years*, words that you might not hear on a daily basis. If you're to be a successful college graduate—or at least sound like one—it's necessary for you to drop these words in normal conversation. If you're keeping track, so far we've got "auxiliary," "propensity," and "nugatory." I'll keep *Webster's* and *Roget's* close by and see what else I can find for us. I might even make up a word every now and then just to make sure you're paying attention.

Second, I keep getting e-mails from parents telling me that their kids didn't get anything out of college and that it was the worst investment they ever made . . . not because of the institution itself, but rather because their charming young lad or lass wasted away four years and has but a mere 8½" x 11" piece of paper to show for it. They partied and met lots of people but didn't embrace the opportunity for a top-notch education. They're proficient at instant messaging and Facebook but wish they'd been more involved on campus. Tons of fun, but an otherwise-wasted experience.

Most important, though, I wish I had read a copy of *The Best Four Years* before I started college. It can be argued that I had a successful and enjoyable college career—indeed, I went to school to play basketball, failed at that, yet still managed some accomplishments off the court along the way. But I can only imagine what life would have been like for me during those four years if I'd had even more direction and motivation. What if I had actually gone to college with a purpose—imagine that—rather than just cruising through? What would I do if I could go back and do it all over again?

That is what this book is about. To give you a little purpose and offer a little direction. It'll be a hard road, but it can be done, and the fact is that you can have a fun *and* successful college experience, if only you know how to play your cards right. This book is your head start.

The Best Four Years is structured so that you can read it however you'd like. You can read it straight through, cover to cover, or you can skip to the sections that are especially appealing to you. Do you want to know a few tips on boosting your grades? Well, flip to chapter 5. Don't want to study abroad? Well then you're missing a great experience, but by all means, disregard that portion of chapter 6.

Whenever I get the hankering to hop on my soapbox and really get all philosophical on you—which tends to happen quite often—I'll box and highlight my thoughts. Get focused and get excited to be enlightened.

I've also been forward thinking enough to include, at the back of this here copy of *The Best Four Years*, several extra blank pages with simply the word NOTES at the top. These pages are to serve one of three purposes (or perhaps all three):

1. Filler pages to make this book appear a few pages thicker than it actually is.
2. Room to write down all the phone numbers, e-mail addresses, and screen names of members of the opposite sex that you will meet while carrying around this book for four years.
3. A place to jot down the most important words of wisdom from the pages of *The Best Four Years*. While this book surely contains all kinds of heavy-duty knowledge, not all of it is for everyone, so you might want to scribble some ideas that are particularly pertinent to your life.

So here it is! College. You're going to be challenged, stressed, triumphant, and gratified. You're going to meet interesting, fun people and grouchy, bitter people. There will be lots of firsts, in all areas of your life, and if you act right, perhaps a few seconds and thirds. There will be people who you'll talk to for the rest of your life and people you hope to never see again. You might even meet that special guy or gal with whom you'll spend the rest of your days. You'll learn more about yourself than you ever did before and more about others than you bargained for. You'll learn (and forget) more than you ever thought possible. You'll procrastinate, you'll cram, and you'll swear it will never happen again. And you'll do it again. You'll get good grades and grades that "just aren't fair." You'll stay up late, wake up early, and nap in the afternoon (although you know you shouldn't). There will be concerts, parties, cultural happenings, and sporting events. Get set to ride an emotional roller coaster, from the highest highs to the lowest lows.

From start to finish, it will be the best four years of your life.

A heap of people would *love* to be in your shoes right now—the same people who thought back, at graduation, on how they would have done things differently along the way. And now here you are with the opportunity and the freedom to choose what to do with your college experience.

What kinds of decisions are you going to make?

The
Best Four
Years

ONE

The Transition

People might tell you, "Oh, boy! Get ready. The move from high school to college is a tough one!" Baloney.

Let's be honest here. You can't wait to get out of your house. And despite all the weeping, your parents can't wait for you to go, either. Dad's going to fire up some candles, and they're going to start sleeping with each other more than they have since the nine months before you were born. Hey, it's the truth. Really. I'll give you a minute to let that digest.

So, the good news is that the transition from high school to college is not a brutal one. Dramatic? Sure. Brutal? Nah. After all, there is no more everyday parental guidance. Nobody is watching over your every move anymore; nobody will be ordering you, "Home by midnight . . . or else!"

On the flip side, though, no one is going to be coddling you, holding your hand, and telling you that everything is going to be A-OK. You're on your own now, for better or for worse.

There are a few tricks and techniques you can use to make the most of your transition and stay one step ahead of those who have come before you. So, sit back, relax, and grab your highlighter. Your first class is in session.

Pack the Essentials

It would be pointless for me to spend any considerable amount of time convincing you what to take with you to college and what to leave at home. I was warned, as were many before me, and we still ended up bringing a carload or two full of stuff we didn't ever use. I packed most everything from my room at home that wasn't wood or didn't have a pulse.

That said, it's important to understand a few things.

First, consider the essentials you use on a daily basis—toothpaste and other toiletries, clothes, your favorite pillow—and then think about why you are going to need any more than that when you get to college. My favorite is when people start shopping for all new stuff a month before leaving home. Why? It's nice to start college off with a new clothes hamper or a new pair of pajamas, sure, but when you start tossing blenders and a new desk chair and a mountain bike into your shopping cart, you're getting carried away. You haven't lifted weights in three months, and now you want to bring those forty-five-pound dumbbells for those late-night urges to do a few sets of curls? And do you really need to bring *To Kill a Mockingbird* and *The Adventures of Tom Sawyer*? Good books, but when are you going to read them? Pack what you know you'll need and buy the rest when you discover you do, in fact, need it *after* you get to school. You'll save time and money, and you'll avoid a cluttered room.

Second, the more you pack, the more ticked off your roommate is going to be when you arrive on campus. More than likely, they're going to overpack, and two or three people stuffed in a cramped dorm room is a recipe for starting the year off on the wrong foot. Space is a luxury in your little alcove, and the more of it you use, the less of it you'll have. (How's that for some knowledge?) The best favor you can do yourself is to make contact with your roommate or roommates ahead of time, before you head off to Wal-Mart. Decide who's going to bring what. She's got a big-screen TV that she absolutely will not leave at home, and you have a kick-ass stereo. Great—there's no need for you to have two stereos or TVs.

Third, don't go nuts with the decoration of your dorm room. "But I'm a girl! I need to decorate, Adam." Right. What I'm telling you is that it can get out of hand and it really isn't that important. Not to mention you'll live in this room for less than a year. Buy some cheap posters, maybe a few Christmas lights, and a fan, and call it a day.

If you're going to splurge on anything, put your dough toward a top-notch laptop (with insurance!). You'll do everything on that laptop, and you want one that will be around for four years, or at the very least, won't crash while you're in the middle of a term paper. Laptop and flip-flops: your two best friends in college. (*Always wear flip-flops in the bathroom!*)

> In the end, as I said, you're going to pack too much. Trust me. But it's cool. Just be prepared to bring it all back home. Or sell it on Craigslist to next year's freshman class.

Homesickness

Okay, as excited as you are to get out of the house and away from the absolute control of your parents, there will be a time—

maybe early on, maybe later—that you will start feeling a little homesick. It's not that you hate college. It's just that you miss your old friends, cafeteria-cooked meals are not Mama-cooked meals, and doing your own laundry in a stuffy room with ten other people just isn't as fun as you thought it would be. You miss home. No worries. It happens. You've made the physical move to college. Now it's time to make the emotional and intellectual move, as well.

Talk It Out

You figured college would be all sunny days, with people trotting around campus, arm in arm, with big cheesy smiles on their faces, just like you saw in the brochures. "Hold up a second. It rains at college, too? And not everybody wants to be friendly toward me? This can't possibly be!"

The good news is that you're not alone. A lot of people on campus are going through what you're going through. So talk about it with your friends. Mention it to your advisor. Meet with a counselor in the health center. (Therapy ain't cheap after college, so take advantage of it now.) Your RA has been there before, and is more than likely dealing with more cases of homesickness than yours, so they'll know how to help you handle it.

You don't have to be geeky about it. "Gosh, I sure miss home. I miss hugging my mom. I miss Sparky. I miss Billy. I miss, I miss, I miss . . ." Just drop it, in casual conversation, that things are going great but that you can't wait to hit up a little bit of Ma's fried chicken (if you live in North Carolina) or some lobster bisque (if you live up in Maine) or an assortment of dairy products (if you hail from Wisconsin). They'll likely be able to relate.

The point I'm getting at: Be open about your feelings. When you call home, discuss the good and the bad aspects of college. When you're talking with your friends, let them know the positive and the negative feelings you are experiencing. They're going through it, too. Bottling it up makes what you're going through only worse, and can lead to more severe situations (like depression—*ugh*).

Get Involved

You can't go home every time you feel homesick. Even if your school is close to home, resist the urge to return on weekends for food and laundry services. Wait at least until Columbus Day to leave the new environment you're trying to create, which will give you a fair shot at adjustment and ease the temptation of falling into your comfort zone. The whole point of college—beyond getting a degree—is for you to get out and make some decisions for yourself, to foster your independence. Having your parents hold your hand along the way won't help.

The best cure for homesickness is to get out and participate in something. Anything. It will help take your mind off why you're homesick in the first place, and it will give you the opportunity to get involved and have a little extra fun on the side. You'll meet new people who have similar interests, and maybe even contribute to a worthy cause that makes a difference in somebody else's life. Imagine that. Cure your homesickness and provide a service to mankind. That's a double play.

Another great cure for homesickness (or stress or depression or bulging hips) is physical exercise. Go for a walk or a jog around campus. Go to the gym. Or even go kick a Hacky Sack with the skaters down at the entrance to your dorm. Whatever you do, you'll feel so much better about yourself when you're done. A healthy body breeds a healthy mind. Plus, it's fun!

Dealing With Mommy and Daddy

Mom and Dad miss you just as much as you miss them. College and your independence are necessary steps, but after the nest has been empty for a month or two—even after they start to get used to you being gone—they miss you. No more Friday-night football games, friends' sleepovers, or bailing you out of the county jail at four in the morning. This is a new experience for everybody.

The best thing you can do is maintain contact—and a good relationship—with your parents. In fact, your relationship with your parents will likely grow to a whole new level with you being away from home. I always had a solid connection to my parents, but when I left home, my pops became one of my best friends. Really. Which is not to say that we talked every day or that I couldn't wait to get home for the summer, but he was there for me through the good times and the bad. Mom, too. She called to wish me luck before tests and games. It was reassuring to know that I was building my own life, yet I still had a connection to my parents that would never go away.

Call your parents, send them letters, and e-mail every now and then, and maybe even include a few pictures. If you become friends with them on Facebook, which might be a horrible idea, make sure to post a picture or two of you studying at your desk to go along with all those pictures of you cockeyed with a red cup in your hand.

Keep in mind that your parents have been there. Maybe they went to college, maybe not. But they've had growing experiences of their own, so they have an idea what you're going through. They can be there for some pretty solid advice that you might not be able to get from an advisor, a counselor, or an RA.

You're in Charge Now

Some people struggle with change. Others thrive on it. If there's one concept that you need to embrace as you move forward into your college career, it is that your life is changing and you are in total control. Now, you can't control what happens to you necessarily, but you can control how you react to all these new situations that are going to arise over the next four years.

This Is a New Beginning, and This Is Exciting!

Probably the most thrilling part of going to college—for me—was that my past was essentially eliminated. I had a brand-new clean slate, and there were no demons to haunt me along the way. No teachers who had heard about me from their colleagues and were just waiting for me to give them a hard time. No ex-girlfriends to spread dirty secrets. *Whew*. It was a brand-new opportunity for me to do what I wanted with my image.

This is it. Your beginning. You asked for it and you got it. This is what you always wanted! Embrace it. Don't let the person you've always been determine who you are going to be now. Build on yourself instead. If you've been a jerk, you don't have to be a jerk anymore! If you've been the coolest kid around and always lent a helping hand to the next guy, you can be even cooler and help even more people now that you're in college. It's great! As I said before, you don't have anybody to answer to. Just you. You don't want to study? Don't study! Don't want to go to class? Don't go! Want to sleep in every day, heat up some Rice-A-Roni for breakfast, and watch TV? Go for it. But it won't go very well, and your college career will be short-lived.

However, if you want to take your life to the next level, right now, then this is your opportunity. Right now! How cool is that? You can learn so many interesting new things; you can participate in clubs, organizations, or student government; you can lose weight; and the whole way through, you can get a great education! You can do whatever the heck you want to! That's pretty flippin' exciting, if you ask me.

Making It on Your Own

The exciting part about all this is that you get to look back on your college experience when you're fifty years old and hold yourself accountable for the decisions you made. Were they good decisions? Bad decisions? Did you make absolutely *no* decisions and just kind of skim the surface without taking any sort of risks?

The summer after your freshman year of college, you're going to have the chance to hang out with some of your old friends. Maybe to your face (but probably behind your back), they're going to say that you've changed. This is a good thing. If you don't change while you're in college—physically, intellectually, emotionally—then somebody wasted a ton of money on you. Change is good! You want change. But you want to change for the better, rather than coming home as some smug ass, walking around town acting as if you're better than everybody else. That's one thing that this book is all about—helping you to avoid becoming a smug ass.

Whatever you do, as you work to foster your growth and development as a person, remain open to new ideas and new opportunities. That, right there, is the key to getting the most out of your college experience. Get out there and meet people. Find some sense of identity for yourself. Develop a set of morals and skills that you can use for the rest of your life. Making it on your own involves embracing the idea that change is going to happen, whether you like it or not. You can't control that. But you can control whether that change is positive or negative.

Having Purpose

If you go to college without a purpose, you're wasting your time and somebody's hard-earned money. You can't expect change and opportunity and good fortune to come to you just because you, your parents, or Uncle Sam is shelling out big bucks for tuition. The problem I see most today is that students are going to college to "find themselves" or "become a man or woman." Which is great. More than likely, it will happen. But you can't go to college without a purpose or maybe even—get this—a few goals. You have to at least know and understand what you're shooting for, at least from a general standpoint—and the rest will sort itself out over the next four years. You can't grasp, right now, what to expect while you're away at college, but you can have an understanding of what you'd like to accomplish.

Now, you can write your goals down all day long. You can paste them on the wall or tape them on the mirror to look at and recite every morning when you wake up. And you can tattoo your purpose on your right bicep so that you and every-body else at the gym are constantly reminded of what you're here for. That's all well and good, except I'm talking about actual action as opposed to talk. Really own your purpose. Represent it every day with the way that you act around your peers and professors. If your purpose or goal is to become a nicer person, then do everything you can, every day, to become a nicer person. If you want to lose weight, then get your act in gear on a serious diet and exercise program. If you want to tackle a research project with one of your professors in an effort to get published, then get after it! It's really a pretty simple concept. You just have to know what you want to accomplish first, and then go out and do it. College is the perfect place to make strides in your life. What do you have to lose?

Expect the Unexpected

If there's one thing you can count on in college, it is that you can't count on anything. Nothing is commonplace across the board. You can read this book ten times before your first day of classes, and you still won't be totally prepared for everything that's going to be thrown at you. Indeed, that's the appeal of college, the allure of going out there, into new, uncharted territory. If the experience was A, B, and C—cut-and-dried—it wouldn't be exciting and it certainly wouldn't be as rewarding.

The best way to embrace the idea of expecting the unex-pected is to go out and take risks. In the end, that's what college is all about. Well, maybe "managing risk" is a better way to put it. It's one thing to take all kinds of stupid risks, but it's another to take sound-minded, calculated risks. Sex without protec-tion? Stupid risk. Stopping by to meet your neighbor when their door is open? Sound-minded risk. Saving a twenty-page research paper for the night before it's due? Stupid risk. Taking your professor out for a cup of coffee to ask them the best way to study for the next test? Sound-minded risk. You get the idea.

Think of yourself as walking around with a bubble around you. I'm asking you to blow that bubble up as big as it will go, starting with your first day of college. Let people in to get to know who you are, and before you know it, your bubble will burst and you won't even care.

The great thing about taking risks is that the more you take, the more you're going to learn what you're good at and what you love, as well as what doesn't work for you. If you join a club and don't like it, drop out. If that hot guy you approached in the cafeteria turns out to be a dud, walk away. Taking chances increases your opportunity for success and happiness, no matter who you are. And college is a great place to start taking those chances.

If you know to expect the unexpected, then you'll be ready when the unexpected hits you. (Or something like that.) Point is, don't go into college thinking you know what's going to happen. You don't. Nobody does. Appreciate that, and you're ahead of most of the other people in your class.

Get Used to Rejection

"Back in '82, I could throw a football over those mountains . . ." Really? Great. Nobody cares. If you were the cool kid in high school, then get used to a brand-new experience, homes. It doesn't work like that in college. Remember that clean slate I was talking about a minute ago? Well that applies to you, too. The high school geeks get a chance to prove themselves just as much as the captain of the cheerleading squad. If you were the star of your high school basketball team, then you're just an average hoopster now. If you dated the hottest guy at Bambam

High School last year, that doesn't mean you're a shoo-in to date the hottest guy this year. You get the idea. You've got to prove yourself all over again.

The trick is to embrace rejection. Prepare yourself for it. If you walk into a situation knowing and understanding that rejection is a very plausible option, you'll exceed expectations no matter what. "My professor conceivably might not like the topic I've chosen for my thesis, but I'm going to go talk to her about it anyway." Don't go in with a negative attitude—load up on all the confidence you can muster—but just understand that rejection is a real possibility.

Pay Your Dues, Just Like Everybody Else

Just as those before you had to earn respect and admiration (or not), you have to, as well. They spent their freshman year making some of the same mistakes you're going to make and then learning some of the same lessons you're going to learn. Deal with it. That's how it's supposed to be. It's all part of the growing process.

Paying your dues applies to all areas of life on the college circuit and beyond. With your social life, you've got to remain humble until you've worked your way into an environment where you're comfortable. With your academic life, maybe you'll take the time to work with a professor on a research project, doing all his grunt work while proving that you have what is necessary to succeed academically. (Hey, you might even learn something along the way.) If you have a job on campus, same thing: you can't expect to make your own hours or be the manager of the school bookstore when other students have been working there for a year or two or three. You gotta pay your dues.

After you have put in the time, then you will start to work

your way up. "Say . . . um . . . Professor Manguson . . . so
. . . uh . . . y'know, I've been putting in a lot of hours working on this research project with you. And . . . um . . . so . . .
like . . . I'm having a great time and all. Maybe, if you think
I've been doing all right, we can add a little extra responsibility on my plate. Whatd'ya think?" When he says, "Yeah,
sure, kid," you should take those new responsibilities very
seriously. Work longer and harder than anybody who ever
worked under him. You bring him lemonade on Tuesday and
flowers on Friday. Finish ahead of schedule and with better
results than he anticipated.

> Overachieve and you pay your dues quicker than the next guy.

Be Yourself and You'll Find Yourself

Sheesh! If there's one thing nobody can stand about one of their
peers—and it's ironic because it happens very, very often—it's
that they act like somebody they're not. They put up a fake
persona, as if there is a standard that must be met and they're
shooting to meet that standard at all costs, when really they just
want to be accepted.

Of course you want to be accepted. Everybody does. But
do you want to be accepted as someone you're not? Be yourself! Shoot. It's more fun that way. You don't have to put up a
façade or wear different personality masks. Just be you. People
will either accept you or not. Who cares really? If they don't
like you, that's their problem, not yours. But if they do like
you, then you know that they like you for you and not because
you're trying to be somebody else.

Now maybe you're thinking that this contradicts what I was saying before about change and taking risks. No question, there is a fine line to tread here. The trick is to hang tight to the values that make you who you are but always keep an eye out on how you can improve yourself as a person. Go out there and discover who you really are. Surround yourself with good, positive people, but don't compromise who you are to be accepted. Please yourself first, and others will follow.

Keep in mind that all this takes time and work. Nothing is easy. Friendships aren't easy. Relationships aren't easy. And it isn't easy to stay true to your values when they are constantly being challenged. It's hard to avoid certain situations, especially when "everybody else is doing it." But that's all part of the process. This is a good thing. You want to be challenged. College is a four-year-long test to see who you are, and if you maintain a high level of integrity while your peers are trading theirs in, then you've already passed.

Roommates

Your roommate is going to be, perhaps, the most important person in your life as you move forward through your college years. Maybe they're exactly the kind of person you want in a roommate: someone to hang out with on the weekends and study with during the week; they bring you Jell-O and ginger ale when you're not feeling so great and go to the gym with you when you are. Or maybe they're the devil's spawn and you just wish they would *go the hell away*. "Is your girlfriend our third roommate, and are those really your dirty socks on my desk?" Either way, they're here to stay (unless you decide to move), so it's important that you learn to make the most out of your relationship.

Sharing

What you choose to share with your roommate is to be determined by the agreements the two (or three or four) of you make, and only time can tell how those will develop. Keep in mind a few things:

- You can save a boatload of money on clothes, DVDs, CDs, textbooks, and other personal items if you choose to share them. At the same time, maybe you're not comfortable letting your roommate borrow your shoes. Fair enough, but make that arrangement known ahead of time in order to avoid any sort of confrontation later. *Avoid conflict later with proactive communication now.*
- Unless (against my advice) you each brought two of every appliance and electronic gadget, his stereo is your stereo and your TV is his TV. Get used to it. It's not that big of a deal. Learn a little bit of discipline and flexibility here. In the end, you might end up liking your roommate's choice of music or television shows.
- You're going to spend the rest of your life sharing, so why not develop good habits now?

Comfort Levels

You can't expect your personality to mirror that of your roommate's and vice versa. Maybe it will or maybe it won't. Who knows? Maybe you have a vibrant outgoing personality, while your roommate is quiet and prefers to keep to himself or herself; or you want to talk about everything that happened today while you were away at classes, and your roommate doesn't. Or maybe you're . . . Really, it doesn't matter. As a matter of fact, it's probably going to be more entertaining if the two of you have opposite personalities that complement each other, rather than having to live with a mirror image of yourself.

Each of you is going to have a different comfort level. They're going to want everything clean and tidy, and you have reserved that space next to your desk for "dirty clothes, et cetera." You want to have lights-out at ten-ish because you have to get up and run through your notes for an eight o'clock class, but his girlfriend just came over at ten-fifteen for another late-night "study session." Establish rules early on (communicate!) to avoid deeper issues later.

With Whom Shall I Room?

Whether it's from personal experience or not, you've heard from your mom, your dad, your advisor, your high school guidance counselor, and your neighbor that it's a bad idea to room with a friend. That, dear reader, is sound advice, especially if that friend is from your high school. After all, you're trying to break free and spread your wings and take your life to new levels. How is an extension of high school going to do that? It doesn't mean you're not friends anymore; you just aren't sleeping in the same room.

I would say probably the best thing to happen to me in college was meeting Bruno and Lightfoot, my two roommates and best friends for the duration of my time at Merrimack. And I wouldn't have had it any other way. I learned more about different cultures than I ever could have anticipated. (Bruno was from Paraguay, and Light was from Sierra Leone.) Even better,

Bruno was this beautiful Latin man, so our dorm room had a revolving door swinging open daily with lovely ladies coming to see him. I met some terrific girls just by my association with him. (Hey, sometimes you just have to settle for seconds.) And with Lightfoot's connections all over campus, I didn't have to buy many textbooks (or Easy Mac or DVDs) starting day one of our freshman year.

Branch out and make your first friend by picking or being assigned a random roommate. You might get along okay if you room with an old friend, but I promise you're eventually going to get sick of each other. Whether your friendship is strong or not, little conflicts will be magnified into overly dramatic, serious ones. And it can only put a damper on your motivation to get out and meet new people. "Why go out? I've got my friend right here!"

Absolutely, most definitely, don't discount your friends from before college. Those can be the best, strongest friendships, the ones that you can keep over the years, through all your developmental changes. Just expand your reach a little. Reach out and meet someone. If you don't like your new roommate, fine. You lose a friend that was never a friend to begin with. But if you bump heads with an old friend while rooming together, you could potentially lose a great friendship.

> Besides, just like with sharing, you're going to have to get used to working with and compromising with a variety of random people in your life, so there are a lot of lessons to be learned right now by living with someone you didn't know before college.

Roommate Friendships Could Last Forever

The toughest part about random roommate pairings is that you never know what's going to happen. On move-in day, you could end up meeting your first college friend or you could despise each other from the get-go. You just don't know.

No matter what, though, don't judge your roommate from the onset. First impressions are lasting impressions, of course, but let's dig a little deeper since you'll be getting a second and a third and a tenth impression. Keep an open mind to the possibility that you could actually learn a whole heck of a lot from them. Keith, my roommate junior year, was probably around four and a half feet tall or so standing on a phone book; I'm pretty sure he'd be considered a midget in certain countries. So, he didn't look like much, but he turned out to be a strong businessman who worked on campus and also ran his own landscaping and snowplowing company. He worked fifty-seven (*fifty-seven!*) hours per week while he was in school (to minimize his post-college debt) and still found time to go to class and stay on top of his schoolwork. He was a hustler, for sure. We talked all the time about budgeting and finance issues, and we shared ideas on a couple business projects for school. If I had judged him for the short man that he was (and still is), I wouldn't have created a lifelong friend and contact in the business world.

After a month or two, once you've had a chance to get to know your new roommate a little bit, you can judge them. By then, you'll have a better picture of who they really are. Maybe you like them and maybe not. Either way, you've given it a shot. If you really, really, *really* can't find it within yourself to put up with their late-night antics or their hygiene or their snoring or their sleeping habits, put in a request to move rooms. You certainly don't need to compromise the rest of your year—

socially, academically, psychologically—for a faulty roommate combination, though it is worth pushing it out for a month or two before you make that decision.

Establish Rules Early

I touched on it before, but it's important that I hammer this issue home, because it is critical that you establish rules with your new roommate or roommates. Even if they are the hippest, most easygoing people on campus, some silly little issue is going to arise and get out of hand, and you don't want it to ruin an otherwise-healthy living situation simply because you didn't take a few minutes to chat things out ahead of time (in person! Which does not include sending instant messages across the room).

So, what type of rules am I talking about here? It really depends on your personal preferences. My roommates and I always had a no-smoking policy in the room (think again if you think that your residence hall is "smoke-free"), and we established rules on cleaning the room, sharing food, and overnight guests. We even arranged times that we could each have a little private time in the room (Bruno and I, with our girlfriends, and Lightfoot, by himself), so there wouldn't be any awkward, embarrassing moments.

Okay, okay. So maybe I'm being a little dramatic here, getting all serious on you with these "rules." Fine. Understand that I'm not saying you need to write out a contract, sign it, and have it notarized. You don't need to post these rules on the door as a colorful poster with star stickers. Calm down. A simple conversation will do. "Hey Lashonda, let's talk a minute. This is kinda silly, but there are a few ground rules I think we should establish as we move forward as roommates.

Whatd'ya think about . . . ?" *Bam.* There you go. It's as simple as that.

If an issue does come up, where (oh, no!) your roommate is in violation of a rule or guideline you each agreed to ahead of time, bring it up immediately rather than letting it linger and build to where it could potentially become more serious. No matter what, you don't want things to blow up because of some small unresolved issue that boils to the surface. Besides, this is for the benefit of each of you. Do you really want to keep taking care of your drunk, high, let's-talk-for-an-hour-about-why-Kristy-hasn't-called-me-back roommate every Wacky Wednesday, Thirsty Thursday, and Freaky Friday just because you don't have the *huevos* to communicate? He needs to get his act together, and you do, too, so help each other out.

> After all is said and done, roommates who want to get along will get along no matter what the situation is. Set the precedent early, though, by communicating a few guidelines to which you both can adhere.

Having a Gay Roommate When You're Not Gay (or Being the Gay Roommate)

This issue is becoming more and more germane today than ever. Yesterday's closet dwellers are out and proud now—as they should be—rather than keeping their sexualities private. So, if you're gay or if you're rooming with someone who is openly gay, be sensitive to the situation that you are both in.

If you're gay, own it! If your friends or your roommate don't accept and support you, screw 'em. They clearly aren't the kind of people you want to surround yourself with anyway. If it gets out of hand, move out and find another roommate with more of an open mind.

If you have a gay roommate, respect their situation. Let go of the stereotypes. You are who you are, and they are who they are. If nothing else, they could use your friendship and support, now more than ever. Besides, this might be a once-in-a-lifetime opportunity to meet and live with someone who is gay, so take the time to become educated and enlightened.

Chapter in Brief

Okey dokey, let's review:

- Pack only the essentials when heading off to college. You don't want to clutter up valuable residence-hall space with blenders and that mountain bike you didn't need after all.
- Deal with homesickness by talking it out with your peers and your family; then go out and get involved around campus. Don't go home every weekend just because you miss your old life.
- You're in charge of your life now. Own it! Take risks and find your passion.
- Get used to rejection. You aren't in high school anymore.
- Roommates come in all shapes, sizes, colors, and personalities. Open the lines of communication, and you'll get along just fine.

TWO

You're All Grown Up Now

I f you're looking for a leg up in college, then here we go. If there is a secret, a magic tip, a golden rule of optimum achievement in college, it is to maximize your productivity by managing your productivity. *Bam.* That's it. But it's not as easy as it sounds, and it sure isn't easy to get started. They say old habits die hard, and this, your first shot at independence, is when that saying is really going to materialize. You're used to tossing your load of dirty clothes in the laundry room for Mom to take care of (at least I was), and Dad has been waking you up every morning at seven forty-five after you hit SNOOZE three times. Those days are over, my friend.

Developing a system—your system—of organization requires trial and error because, after all, your friend Susie may have a similar way of doing things as Todd, and while their system might work for them, it might not be the most effective way for you to get things done. Find your system of organization, and you'll find success in college.

Time Management

Sure, it can be argued that college is independence with a safety net. More than likely, your parents or your close friend Martin or Uncle Pudge are just one phone call away. At the very least, you're a short saunter over to a counselor or the school administration building. You're not totally thrown into the wild here. Somebody's there for you just in case of an emergency.

But that's it. Emergency. If you're picking up the phone whenever you need something or trotting around campus laying responsibilities on all your resources, then what the heck are you in college for in the first place? Own your life, babe. It's time to start making decisions for yourself. No more hand-holding. No more turning to others for routine assistance. Today is the first day of the rest of your life as your own person. Yay!

The first decisions you make—indeed, the decisions you make before you even make the decision to start making decisions—need to revolve around time management. College is time management.

You Can Fool Me, but You Can't Fool Yourself

The reason it's easy to waste time in college is that there is such a surplus of it. Think about it. You go to class fifteen hours or so a week. That's it. Really, that's the only aspect of attending college that is mandatory. So in between going to class, you have all kinds of free time to fill with everything else: studying, going to club meetings or outings, eating, sleeping, working, and writing on your friends' Facebook walls. Those idle hours outside class can work for you or against you, depending upon how you spend them.

The only person who really cares (or should care) about how

you spend those idle hours is you. Your roommate doesn't care if you sleep all day long. Your advisor doesn't care if you study; she won't be calling to look after you unless you're treading the line of flunking a class (or just flunking out altogether)—and maybe not even then! Your parents' main concern is that you walk across the stage in four years. And your friends won't care if you haven't hit the gym in two weeks or if you dart for the burger section of the cafeteria every day for lunch. They don't care one way or the other. They'll just talk about you when you're not around. "Damn, homeboy's growin' horizontally, isn't he?"

But you should care. This is your life, and this is your time. You don't have to prove anything to anybody but yourself. Seize that idea. It's great (and important) to form support groups and to have a clique of friends who look out for one another's interests, but at the end of the day, the only person you have to answer to is you. And that was the scariest aspect of college for me personally—that I had all this time to do whatever the heck I wanted to. And nobody's watching. I can remember having some super-productive get-the-heck-out-of-my-way-I'm-coming-through-type days, and I can remember days where—well, I don't really remember what I got done. I can also remember how I felt at the end of each of those days. Think about the productivity in your past life, before college. Don't you feel more gratified when you lay your head down on your pillow after a constructive, worthwhile day as opposed to a day where you were merely a waste of space?

Now, don't get it twisted here. It's cool to take it easy sometimes, too. And you absolutely should. Everybody deserves a vacation. There are only twenty-four hours in a day, so there is a limit to what you can accomplish. If you just put in three hard days of reading for English, studying for a philosophy exam, and researching and writing a lab report for chemistry and you're planning to go hard again this fourth day, be careful, and take a step back to evaluate how you're feeling. College is tough and is supposed to challenge you to the limit—true—but you don't want to get burned out. I've seen it happen to the best scholars around. Top-notch in high school; overload and crash in college. You don't want to be too much of a machine. Take it easy every once in a while.

Just don't forget why you're in college in the first place. Don't forget that nobody's really watching you.

Don't Procrastinate

We'll talk about this later. I'm going to go watch a movie and maybe grab a nap.

Maximize the Little Breaks

The fifteen- to twenty-minute or hour-long breaks between classes that you consider to be superfluous or insignificant can actually be the key to your success in college. You can go to the library or your favorite secluded spot and pick up an extra two to four hours per day of study, research, writing, and reading time during those breaks. Two to four hours! You might not ever have to study at night again. Okay, maybe that's an exaggeration (or maybe not), but you get the idea. Think about what you can accomplish in short study bursts rather than waiting until the end of the day for an exhausting marathon study session. Your brain can take only so much at one time, so short breaks every thirty minutes actually optimize your time. Sitting around doing nothing or napping (*ugh*, more on that shortly) or seeing what your friends are up to on Facebook can be the burglars of time.

What you're trying to do here is ride the momentum of the day. Once you get two things done, you'll be fired up for the next. Don't even return to your room at all during the day if you can help it. There are too many diversions there that can draw your attention away from an otherwise-productive day. Once you're out, stay out. You can use this time for so many other things. Run to the store to pick up school supplies. Go to the gym. Eat. Meet with a professor. Just do something productive in between classes! When you come back at the end of the day, you'll be riding a high from everything you were able to accomplish.

> Discover what's best for you. What is your best method of time management? What works best for Paul or Claudette—who like to wake up and study early in the morning—might not work best for you. Fine. But you're not Paul or Claudette. Find your own time-management system.

Schedule, Schedule, Schedule

Did I mention the word "schedule"? If you ask ten different people their thoughts on scheduling, you're going to get a variety of answers. Some will say that you should be writing out daily to-do lists and crossing items off as you accomplish them. Doesn't it feel great at the end of the day to look at a list of items that you've spent the day scribbling through? Ah, what productivity! Even as I write this, crossing lines off my outline makes me feel pretty awesome. Others, though, would argue that a failed to-do list brings out the mentality that it's a failed day. "I got only eight out of ten things completed. What a waste of a day." While there are pros and cons to scheduling, most can agree that it's important to have some sort of organization to the day ahead. Even with the unpredictability of the time required to complete certain tasks and assignments ("I can't believe that paper took me three friggin' hours!"), have an idea what direction you're headed.

Scheduling also relieves stress. Attacking an organized day gives you a better picture of where you're headed. If you're grinding hard on a project and you know you've scheduled free time with Herbert for later, it gives you something to work toward. When you're relaxing, you know that you already worked your butt off, so it puts your nerves at ease and allows you to enjoy that leisure time with your friends.

> Schedule your class time; schedule your work time; schedule your free time. Schedule *all* your time and you gain peace of mind.

To-Do or Not To-Do

If you ask me, to-do lists are great. I spent my whole college career working off to-do lists. In fact, I thrived off them because accomplishing one task would boost me up and get me ready for the next. It was like a scavenger hunt I planned for myself each morning. Before I knew it, my list was complete and I'd still have hours left to burn in the day. If you're the kind of person, though, who gets flustered and frustrated when all tasks aren't completed at the end of the day (rather than simply carrying them over to the next day, as sane people do), it might be better to amend the traditional to-do list system a bit.

Try this: Every morning, take out a scratch piece of paper and write out your class and appointment schedule. Then off to the side, make two to-do lists. One is a list of imperative tasks that must be completed immediately:

- Buy toothpaste
- Call car-insurance agent
- Read chapters 6–8
- E-mail Professor Morton to request a letter of recommendation

Your second list is an ongoing list of sorts, less important tasks, but still tasks that you can work on in your free time:

- Write outline for English comp essay
- Work chest and abs at the gym
- Call Ma and Pa

If you're managing your time effectively (and you are, because you're paying attention to *everything* I'm writing to you), you'll get all your tier-one tasks done without issue and you'll make a worthwhile dent in your second list. Either way, you won't throw a fit if your day gets thrown a curveball and you don't get everything done. Tasks that don't get completed simply get carried over to the next day.

The reason to-do lists were so effective for me throughout college is because I tend to be a tad scatterbrained. I'll get going with the day, and before I know it, it'll be lunchtime and I'll be wondering what it was that I was supposed to remember to do. A quick glimpse at my to-do list gets me back (and keeps me) on track. And it takes only two minutes in the morning.

> Don't go overboard making your to-do list. I know some list lovers who take it to the extreme:
> [*]Put shoes on
> [*]Eat breakfast
> [*]Go to bathroom
> [*]Feed dog
> [*]Empty trash
> [*]Brush teeth
> [*]Make to-do list for the afternoon
> No way. Your to-do list is for items beyond the obvious.

Don't Overestimate Your Free Time

One of the common mistakes made on college campuses involves overestimating how much time you have to get things done in the day. By the time you eat, work out, go to class, and hang out with your boyfriend for an hour in the afternoon, it's dinnertime and you're wondering how all that white space on your calendar got filled with menial tasks. Don't take free time for granted and don't assume that you can just "squeeze everything in this afternoon." Be realistic about your plan for the day. You can't possibly fit three hours' worth of studying in between Spanish and English lit, so use that time to crank out a couple of pages on a research paper.

No matter how hard you plan, though, some random situation is inevitably going to arise, which, if you let it, could throw off your entire day. Be open to trading time. If you're working on a paper that isn't due until the day after tomorrow and your friends invite you to a movie that is open for only one more night, go for it. Just be mindful to weigh the importance of the tasks you're trading. If you go to the movie tonight, you're still going to have to work on that paper tomorrow night instead of going to see the band that is coming to campus.

Remember that the more you get accomplished earlier in the day, the more free time you will have later. Use that as motivation. "I can conceivably get all this done by four o'clock and then watch TV and eat Fritos for the rest of the evening." Work hard now; relax later. *Delaying gratification*—in the short term and long term—is a great practice to develop for college, and forever.

Batching Tasks

The easiest and most effective (and most important) way to structure your daily schedule is to batch the tasks that need to be completed, which can be done in a variety of ways. You can batch your tasks according to location ("I can eat, work out, get my mail, and stop by Donna's office, all while I'm in the student center"); time ("I can run to the grocery store and stop by the administration building between Philosophy and French"); or importance ("I absolutely have to read chapter 14 and get a case of Diet Dr. Thunder before I can do anything else").

Multitasking is the only way to accomplish many things in a limited amount of time. While you're sitting in that stuffy laundry room waiting for the cycle to end, review your notes for tomorrow's big test. While you're waiting for the bus, crank out a chapter's worth of reading. *Always carry your notes or a book with you.* You'll find yourself getting caught up waiting on something or someone at some point throughout the day, and you'll be glad you can get caught up on assignments or chores you'd rather not do later.

Be smart about how you batch and multitask, though.

Watching TV while reading won't be effective, nor will trying
to iron your laundry while munching on pizza. Instead, iron
your laundry while you watch TV and down the pizza while
reading. (Wait, are you really ironing your laundry in college?
Seriously?)

Batching, above all, gives you the opportunity to look at the
smaller picture. If you spend your time thinking about all the
things you have to accomplish by next week, you'll feel overwhelmed. Instead, focus on the immediate tasks at hand.
That doesn't mean blowing off bigger projects or long-term
assignments, but use batching as a way to chip away at them
rather than throwing those small blocks of time away.

Scheduling Needs Versus Wants

Of course, your intention, when you tear out that piece of
scratch paper and start scribbling out your to-do list in the
morning, is to get everything done. It all sounds good at 8 a.m.
"Oh boy, this is just going to be the greatest day *ever*! I'm going
to do this and this and this, and—oh wait—can't forget that!"
Right. As I said, *sounds* great.

You have to be realistic, taking the time to schedule a balance of wants and needs. It's not smart—or effective—for you
to schedule all wants ("I'm going to work out, run to the mall,
and then hang out with Becky") or all needs ("I've got to read
for Communications class, study note cards for Trig, and write
up the lab report for Biology"), or to inundate yourself altogether with too much of each ("Before two o'clock, I'm going
to work out, run to the mall, hang out with Becky, read for

Communications class, study note cards for Trig, and write up the lab report for Biology").

In college, there are three areas of your life that you need to manage before anything else: schoolwork, health, and your job. They should be at the forefront of your priorities, before you start worrying about what to wear to which party or which trip to plan.

A job might not be as important to you (especially once you turn twenty-one and that trust fund starts kicking out checks) as it is for someone else (who is paying for tuition with tips earned bartending at your local watering hole), but if you do have one, take it seriously. Mind your employer's demands, but if your job gets too burdensome, find a different one. This added stressor can take only a negative toll on your schoolwork and your health. But a job, which can be fun and productive and keep you motivated and out of trouble, can be a very good thing beyond just putting money in the bank.

Schoolwork and health, as you will discover by the end of your first semester, go hand in hand. If one teeters, the other will knock it down. If you begin to slack with your studies, you'll alter an otherwise physically and mentally sound state of being that could see you gaining (or losing) weight and getting stressed. Staying healthy—from both a mental and a physical standpoint—is just as important to your success in college as your study habits. Read, write, study, eat well, and work out. If you start to falter, get help from an RA or a counselor. After all, your tuition is paying their salaries in the first place.

There are a hundred things you're going to want to do every week. It's the curse of college—too much going on, not enough time to fit it all in. You're never going to have enough time to attend all the extracurricular activities, sporting events, concerts, or social gatherings going on around campus, but it's not as difficult as you think to harmonize your wants with your needs. It's give and take. When you're studying, what are you giving up that you want to be doing? And is it worth it? Vice versa: instead of going to watch your favorite band, should you be studying for Friday's big history exam? Rank the pros and cons of what you're giving up and what you're gaining by doing what you're doing. You don't feel totally prepared for Friday's test, but this is the *only* time your favorite band is going to be in the area. What's a person to do? (Answer: You go to the concert, but sacrifice Juanita's Thursday-night fiesta to the study gods.) Give and take, homes.

Get a Planner, Keep a Calendar

An unfair, yet pertinent, question college graduates often consider is, If you could go back to college all over again, what would you do differently? It's unfair because nobody should live life with regret, but pertinent because everybody would change something if they could go back. For me, if I could go back and change one thing, I would have scheduled my life better by buying a planner and keeping a calendar.

So far we've looked mainly at the short-term picture of keeping track of what's going on in your life. You're starting to get an idea of what your routine might look like. However, if you neglect the bigger picture—looking days, weeks, even months ahead—you'll find yourself bogged down with all kinds of commitments that you "totally forgot about." Don't let that happen. Plan your semester, and you're planning for success.

I *know* you already bought a planner or organizer. I know you did. At the very least, tell me you're planning (yes, I intended that pun; in fact, I've been waiting for six days to use it) on buying one as soon as you finish this chapter. It can be a tad intimidating walking through the calendar-planner aisle at Wal-Mart, but don't get flustered. Calm down. Breathe. Do your Lamaze. Buy a planner based on your own scheduling style. Do you want a weekly-daily planner combo that you can use for everything? Or do you want something simpler to plan the bigger tasks and then just use a piece of scratch paper for your daily itinerary? Do you want a pocket planner or a dry-erase wall calendar to hang next to your desk? Or both? Ah! Overload! It doesn't matter. Just get something that will work for you. (Most university handbooks, by the way, have a planner in them, and they're free.)

(A sidenote: I don't recommend getting an electronic planner or keeping your schedule in your phone for several reasons: 1. You're going to lose your phone at some point during college, and you don't want to be losing the rest of your life right along with it. 2. If you drop it and it breaks, or the battery dies, or it just crashes altogether, you're left to rely on your memory for *everything* you plugged into your e-calendar. 3. It's really not as easy to use—making additions in the margins or crossing out items you've completed, for example—as a good ol'-fashioned paper-and-pen combination. [The United States spent tens of millions of dollars developing a pen that would write in space; the Russians took up a pencil. Keep It Simple, Stupid.])

On Sunday, as you're getting in the right frame of mind for the week ahead, grab your calendar and sketch out an idea of the major assignments you need to be working on during that week. Your Spanish project isn't due for two weeks, but you should probably get moving on it. Write that down. You have an econ exam next Monday, but it's probably not a good idea to wait until next weekend to start studying for that test. Write that down. You have two major papers due on Friday. Write them down. Then, throughout the week (starting Monday morning), you can break these major assignments into smaller scheduled tasks using your planner or a piece of scratch paper, as I discussed a moment ago. (Full disclosure: My freshman year, I used the back of my hand as my planner in college, which was a stupid move. I looked like a fool, and I often had trouble reading what I had written, especially on Tuesdays and Fridays, when I showered. I saw a dramatic difference when I started using a real planner sophomore year.)

The most important facet of planning your week is that it will keep you from getting lazy or lost. By holding yourself accountable for your responsibilities, you can't possibly go wrong, but if you don't keep a calendar, one forgotten duty can throw the rest of your week off-kilter. ("Dammit! I already missed turning my Microeconomics paper in on time. The rest of this week is gonna suck.")

It might not be a bad idea to assemble and look through each of your syllabi at the beginning of the semester as soon as you get them. That way, you have a general picture of the major papers, projects, and exams that are spread throughout the semester. Then, at the middle of the week, take a look at what you have coming up the following week. Monday can come pretty flipping fast if you're looking at next week's schedule on Saturday.

Keeping a calendar or a work journal, which is *oh so* simple to do and requires little effort on your part, allows you to keep track of your life as a whole and not simply a series of tasks. Your academic life will be more organized, no doubt, but you'll also be more in touch with yourself. Your relationships will be stronger. You'll be more reliable. People will come to understand that they can count on you. Scheduling your life can be the most powerful statement you make—for yourself and others—as you move forward in your college career.

Organize the Life Around You

Time management is huge. Schedule, schedule, schedule. But if you don't have any sort of organization to the rest of your life, you'll still find yourself lacking productivity and becoming less and less efficient as the semester progresses. Like the title of this chapter suggests, you're all grown up now. Your maid service didn't make the trip with you to college, and you now have way more on your plate than you ever had before. That's the bad news. Good news is that it's kind of exciting if you think about it: chicks dig guys who are organized, and guys love a woman who can fend for herself.

Make Your Bed; Clean Your Room

In high school, you had to clean your room only if somebody was coming over. On a good day, you might have stacked a few books on your desk or tossed your covers over your bed as you were exiting the room, in hopes that La Santa de la Clutter would come in behind you and tidy up. Just like time management—and, well, everything else in college—you don't really have to clean your room. Do you want to leave old pizza boxes and dirty clothes scattered about (your section of) the room? Go for it. There aren't any rules in college against a messy room, unless you're absolutely outrageous and your untidiness presents a fire hazard.

But, if you make your bed immediately after you wake up, which takes about thirty seconds a day to do the right way, you're saying to yourself (and your roommates and everybody who visits your room) that you care, that today is going to be a great day. More than that, keeping a clean room leads to more productivity in your life. Here's why: It's very easy to lose focus and get bogged down by the chaos and disarray around you, both emotionally and physically. "Geez, this place is a mess. And where the heck is my blue ballpoint pen?" Conversely, a clean room can keep you going, keep you motivated. "Okay, I just studied for French, wrote an essay for English, found my blue ballpoint pen, *and* my room's clean? I'm on fire! What's next?"

Make it a habit to keep your room clean. Brush your teeth, shampoo your hair, make your bed, empty the garbage, et cetera. Habit. Routine. You can spend two fewer minutes surfing the web each day and have your room spotless. Really, once it's already clean, keeping it clean—by merely stacking books on the shelves where they belong and tossing your dirty laundry in the hamper—is a cinch. Even a thorough cleaning, like dusting and scrubbing the floors once every couple of weeks, will be an easy chore if done regularly.

A dorm room lacking organization is a life lacking organization. (I'm pretty sure the Buddha said that. Maybe it was Confucius.) Besides, when your mom comes to visit, she'll be proud to know she raised a son or daughter who can keep a clean living space.

Decorate Your Room

I know some of you didn't buy my argument in the last chapter about buying "some cheap posters, maybe a few Christmas lights, and a fan, and calling it a day." You're one of those people who absolutely has to have your room decorated more sophisticatedly (yes, that's a word; I just looked it up) than your neighbor. News will spread throughout campus and people will come from all around to see what you've done. And it's not just girls. The most elaborately decorated room I ever saw was during my junior year, where a couple of dudes had created an absolute shrine, complete with home-built shelves that displayed all kinds of artsy-fartsy little trinkets and with a fifty-gallon fish tank. Their place was a hot spot. Everybody loved coming to their room just to sit and admire the shrine. (I imagine it might still be there. Disassembling that wall would have been a shame.)

Fair enough. You want your room decorated. Cool, I get it. But you won't get any advice from me. Want to color-coordinate a few paintings with the lampshades, curtains, rug, and towels? More power to you. Really. I'm not being sarcastic. I think that's great. I never wanted to take on the added time or expense, but it might have been a good idea. The décor in my room, each year, was bland and boring. Still is. I didn't care then, and I care less now.

My college girlfriend, Courtney, knows about decorating rooms, though. She does it well, and she does it on a budget. It takes a lot to get your ex-girlfriend to guest-write a piece for your book (oh, the hoops I've jumped through), so you know that the recommendations she has to offer are on point. Here's Courtney:

> When it comes to making a dormitory space your own in an effort to showcase your personality, think carefully before throwing up posters of every up-and-coming band or celebrity. If you love Kings of Leon, then by all means, pin the Followill boys up. You'll be spending copious amounts of time in your room, so it should definitely reflect your personality, but subtly, not desperately. Think about what the primary function of your room is going to be—people have different priorities and lifestyles, so decorate according to what suits you. Are you matchy-matchy? Call your roommate in advance and figure out a color scheme. Aiming to be the hostess with the mostest? Then invest (wisely

and carefully) in comfortable furnishings and quality audiovisual equipment for entertaining guests. Prefer the comfort of your room to holing up in a quiet corner in the library? Hit up Staples, grab fun organizational supplies, and set up your room to make it favorable for study (i.e., a comfortable chair and minimal distractions). Even if you are not prone to caring about spicing up white walls, making a dorm room your own personal space, somewhere you can decompress and relax, is good for your well-being.

That said, too often (I myself fell victim) students arrive on campus armed with a surplus of pictures, posters, and alcohol paraphernalia, with the intent of suffocating the white walls. Everything from my bedroom at home (including, among other things, a bookshelf, books I would never read in my free time, every yearbook I possessed, and picture frames with no place to stand) stacked up against the hallway walls of my freshman dorm as my roommate and I tried to arrange the room so we could jam everything in. Our space ended up being a cluttered distraction. The next fall, as a savvy sophomore, I took the road less traveled. I left behind my third pair of sneakers; the fifth picture frame, which took up too much desk space; and that pair of jeans I swore would fit me if I lost just five pounds. In turn, my life was much less a hassle come May, when it was time to pack up and ship out for the summer.

In summary, when it comes to decorating, go by the credo less is more. Consider the fact that you are sharing a small space with another person (or people) and try to make a list of what you must have. To be cost-efficient, pick a bedspread, curtains, and other décor that will last you all through the four-year experience (i.e., don't go with the neon-green duvet if you know you'll tire of it after two months). Stay true to your taste and have fun—it will definitely get you amped up for college!

Laundry

Doing laundry isn't fun. Few people get excited or look forward to lugging, cleaning, drying, and folding clothes, but it's just one more of those necessary college evils that you have to keep up with. *Ugh*, all this responsibility!

There are five keys to getting your laundry done as effectively as possible:

1. Don't let it stack up by waiting until you're down to your last pair of socks.
2. Separate the darks from the whites. Maybe you notice an immediate difference or maybe not, but over time, washing them together will only expedite fading.
3. Everybody does their laundry on Sunday afternoons, so try to pick a time when there's less risk that all the machines will be taken. Weekdays during the day are ideal. Or Saturday night around midnight.
4. Even though you're pinching pennies, don't try to save money by stuffing the machines to the brim with a load and a half of dirty clothes. It's useless and ineffective. They can't clean (or dry) if they barely have room to spin.
5. Pay attention to the care instructions on the clothing labels. As a general rule, use cold or lukewarm water for colors and hot water for whites or heavily soiled items.

Of course, there is always the chance that some laundry bandit will come through with his basket and—whether by accident or on purpose—make off with your loot. It might not ever happen to you (never happened to me), but it's a risk you take if you decide to leave your laundry alone. You can avoid this situation altogether by taking a book or notes with you to the laundry area for a couple hours of studying. At the very least, though, periodically check to see if your clothes are done. Leaving a completed cycle the washer or dryer will only irritate your fellow residents, and they will not hesitate to take your load out, toss it to the side, and start their own load.

Ironing

When you pack for college, pack wrinkle-resistant clothes that you don't have to iron.

Manage Your Relaxation

Finding extra time in college is rarely a chore, but if you let loose with pointless idle activities, you risk getting behind on everything else you're working so hard to accomplish. String together a few meaningless endeavors, and it'll be lunchtime, and you'll wonder where your morning went. "Wow. That's pretty incredible. I haven't done *anything* worthwhile since I woke up this morning!"

Eat Alone Sometimes

Some people you meet and spend time with in college will be your pals forever. Over the next four years, you'll go to games and concerts and take trips with them on the weekends. And you'll spend many a meal eating alongside them. Which is fun and necessary. Some of the most enlightening (and heated) conversations of my college career were in the cafeteria. It's not a good idea, though, to spend *every* meal hanging out with your friends. Before you know it, forty-five minutes or an hour has passed and you've long been done polishing off that delicious cafeteria food.

Eating alone once in a while also provides you with a much-needed, albeit momentary, escape of sorts from the realities and stresses of the college world. This solitary time allows for reflection and for the organization of your life. Gather your thoughts. Manage your schedule. "Okay, what have I done? What am I doing? What's going on in my life?" I got some of the best ideas while I was eating by myself at Merrimack. Indeed, that's how I developed the premise for my first book, *Scratch Beginnings*.

Generally, dinner is the meal you'll eat with your friends, just because most people tend to eat breakfast on the go and class schedules are too scattered to synchronize for lunch. That works out perfectly because the last meal of the day is when you can unwind and prepare for a possible second wind studying in the library or doing whatever you happen to be up to that evening.

There's a time to socialize and a time to be by yourself. Maybe you eat alone once a day. Maybe twice. You be the judge, and keep in mind that college is about balancing your social, academic, and extracurricular lives.

Organize Your E-life

All these fantastic technological advances—which I can't list here, lest they become obsolete by the time I go to printing—can work for or against you while you're trying to be as productive as possible in college. The newest cool gadget can work wonders for efficiency, of course, but what happens if it takes over your life and you spend *all* your time checking e-mails or playing games? Is it really healthy for your friendships if you're spending all your time texting (each other, while you're walking side by side)?

Have some discipline. Detach yourself, to a certain degree, from technology. Learn not to spend all of your time on your phone or PDA. Or on the computer. Or with headphones glued in your ears. My goodness, if there's one black hole of time on every college campus (and there is), it's all the Internet applications that you really could go without. I can remember nights in my dorm room when I spent two hours instant messaging people around campus and back home. I'm talking about absolutely meaningless conversations, a sure waste of time: "Hey, what're you up to? . . ." "Nothin', you? . . ." "Nothin' . . ." "Oh, cool . . . How's Courtney? . . ." "Good . . . How's Kara? . . ." "Good . . ." "Oh, cool." And it goes on and on like that for forty more minutes with minute-long lulls so that you can check who wrote on your wall on Facebook. Meaningless. Devoid of any substance whatsoever.

Listen, I love Facebook. I think it's a great (and useful) social tool. It's a way to easily keep up with what your friends are up to. All 2,757 of your closest friends. Go look me up and put in a friend request. I'll probably confirm it by tonight. We can be BFFs. Just don't send me some virtual snowball or love-compatibility test. You can follow my progress, where I've been, and where I'm headed. You can read "25 Things About Me." We'll keep tabs on each other's relationship statuses. Oh, and pictures! *Yay, pictures.* There are photos of me on there white-water rafting and of Ali and Shannon shaving my legs freshman year. Kind of disturbing, actually.

Point is, you can't let all of these fun gadgets and applications run your life. Go online, catch up with a few people, shoot some ideas back and forth about your group business project, and then get off and get back to what's important . . . life! Real human contact—or at least a phone conversation—is more significant anyway. You don't want to look back on college and think about all the time you wasted alone in your room, enslaved to the Internet Beast. Live your life offline. Expand your comfort zone and get out and meet people. Don't miss these moments.

More important, though, job recruiters across the country are complaining more and more about the faulty communication skills of today's graduates. So many botched interviews just because we spend so much time stuck to the computer that we can't communicate like normal people. Not to mention the roommate conflicts that arise because Sally wrote on Mary's wall that she looked "phat," and Mary thought she meant "fat," and now she needs a new roommate. *Ugh.*

Oh yeah, that reminds me. Be careful what you post. If you're nineteen and you have pictures of you with a Bud Light in your hand, it can be held against you. You don't think college administrators have Facebook? *Ha.* They're policing outlaws from the comfort of their office chairs. Sneaky buggers. And if you're a leader on campus (or are trying to be), how do you think it looks when you post a hateful comment about someone who crossed you? Facebook—and all these other social utilities—are public domains. Be mindful of who's out there.

If you think back to the section on batching, you can really apply those techniques here. Devote (limit!) thirty minutes of your day to your e-life. Empty your in-box, download a couple songs, and log on to Instant Messenger and Facebook. Thirty minutes a day. Then splurge at 2 a.m. Sunday morning and write drunken messages that you'll regret when you wake up.

Okay, I'm off my soapbox. Now, back to your regularly scheduled programming.

Sleep Right

Your snooze button, just like the Internet, is another one of those aggressive time cheaters that can have you wondering where your day has gone. The fact that you can sleep all day long (on Saturday and Sunday, in particular) doesn't mean it's a good idea. Oversleeping can be a waste of time and can actually leave you drowsier and with less energy throughout the day than if you got your prescribed eight hours (or six or seven or whatever it takes for you to function properly). Not getting enough sleep is just as unhealthy and can take its toll on your body (and your productivity) in the long run as you work to fight off fatigue. Find the sleeping consistency that keeps you enlivened throughout the day.

A quick pointer on sleeping: If possible, start your day fast in the morning, and slowly progress to less grueling activities in the evening. Not only does this ease the stress of your day but it also enables you to begin to relax before you go to sleep in the evening, which is a key tactic to getting a good night's sleep.

No matter how you decide to budget your time under the covers, though, sleeping right involves never doing two things . . .

Don't Nap

I love naps. Oh boy, do I love naps. They feel so good. Nothing beats a siesta after you've been working hard since eight that morning.

Bad idea. Horrible, actually. For a bunch of reasons.

Napping interrupts your sleep pattern. When you nap, rarely do you satisfy the full cycle of the stages of sleep (REM and non-REM), so you're not doing yourself or your body any favors. Napping also kills momentum. You'll be doing great things all day long and then, all of a sudden—*bam!*—you come crashing down to zero productivity by taking a nap. And napping rarely provides the intended effect anyway. Generally, you wake up more sluggish and less energized than before you laid your head down on your pillow.

Instead of napping, try going out for some exercise or to run some errands. Load up on fresh fruit, which is a natural stimulant. In any event, avoid needing a nap by getting a good night's sleep in the first place. If you're tired, push it out for a few more hours and get to bed early so you'll wake up ready to go in the morning.

Don't Pull All-Nighters

If you've been paying attention *at all* throughout this chapter, you'll never need to pull an all-nighter. You won't have to because you'll be managing your time and planning your assignments so effectively in the first place that there'll be nothing left to do at the end of the day. Besides, it's hard to accomplish anything in the middle of the night, when your eyelids are sagging and you're merely shuffling paper around your desk. Go to bed and get up early tomorrow morning, geared up to make things happen (rather than spending tomorrow in a trance because you were up the whole night).

Also, be conscious that caffeine is, in fact, a drug. Be wary of depending on pills or pots of coffee to keep you awake or to jump-start your day. It's addictive, and it's not good for you.

The first time you save an assignment for the night before it's due and you have to stay up all night working on it, you'll see what I'm talking about. And you'll swear it will never happen again.

Chapter in Brief

Okey dokey, let's review:

- Your time is your responsibility now. Manage your time effectively so you don't find yourself scrambling to catch up on chores and assignments that could have already been done. Stop procrastinating. Maximize the little breaks so you'll have less to do later.
- Schedule your life. Schedule what's important, and schedule what's not so important. Schedule everything. Schedule, schedule, schedule. Buy a planner or a calendar. Take two or three minutes in the morning to make a list of the day's tasks.
- Organize the life around you. Make your bed; clean your room; do your laundry.
- Managing your relaxation means effectively managing the idle moments of your day. Mind your Internet usage. Sleep right, and don't nap or stay up all night.
- Key word: *manage*. Be the manager of your life!

THREE

Days of Destitution

There's a touch of irony to your financial situation in college. After all, you've enrolled in college in an effort to build a financial safety net for your future. With a degree from an institution of higher education, you will be armed with the ability to do far more with your life—financially and otherwise—than if you'd stayed at home and stuck it out with just a high school diploma. With a college degree and a little ambition, you're going to make big bucks one day.

But that day is not today. And it's not tomorrow. And more than likely, unless you score some primo internship or Mommy and Daddy are sending you "meal money" ("Dear Mom and Dad, College is great. Please send funds soon for food and additional school supplies. Love, Adam"), it's not going to be anytime over the next four years. So, here you are in college, pumped to take your life to the next level and get paid big bucks, and you're going to be more broke than you've ever been in your life. If you were broke in high school, then, my goodness, get ready for a brand-new low.

It's not all bad, though. If nothing else, you're going to get a taste of the simple life. You'll learn some valuable financial lessons while you're in college (I hope). When you go out to eat or to a concert or to a club, you're going to be mindful of the money you spend. You'll learn to calculate 20 percent gratuities to the penny. Generic brands, the status symbol of college, are going to clean you, hydrate you, do your hair, cure your ailments . . . basically carry you through college. Tide is now CVS-brand laundry detergent; Mountain Dew is now Mountain Lightning; and all your over-the-counter medicines are now made by some pharmaceutical company named Equate. Your entire life, let alone your social life, is going to be on a budget. Which is great. It is now officially "cool" to boast about how much you got for a little. And best of all, when you graduate, you're going to have the right mind-set to make some good decisions (I hope) with your first fat paycheck.

So what's a person to do to survive on meager means during college? Let's indulge ourselves, shall we?

Working

Whether you decide to get a job during the semesters is up to you. If your parents are sending you money, you might not need a job. If you worked your buns off this summer and saved money for the school year, you might not need a job. If you are donating plasma twice a week—well, that's a job. Either way, if you're aiming to keep up with your friends on the weekend and to keep your desk stocked with a healthy supply of pens and pencils and paper clips, it might be a good idea to pick up a little extra cash wherever you can.

Get a Worthy Job

Your motivation to get a job in college can extend beyond the common ideology that you have to make as much money as possible in as short a time as possible. That's obviously not going to happen anyway. Beyond an extra paycheck, though, an on-campus (or even an off-campus) job can bring much-needed organization and cohesion to an otherwise-turbulent life.

Some people look for the easiest job on campus, the slacker job that they overheard an upperclassman talking about in the student union. "Dude, I work for the Campus Copy Center. My man, I'm tellin' you, we don't do anything all day. It's great. I just get to sit around." Even for an overachiever like yourself, this might be the job you're looking for, though not because you get to slack off. If you can find one of those lazy sit-and-watch-the-grass-grow-type jobs (no, they're not reserved just for star athletes), you can put yourself in a position where you get paid *and* get to do schoolwork at the same time. Every now and then, you kick a bunch of copies out of the copier or you go for a delivery run around campus or you shelve a few books, but for the most part, slacker jobs give you the freedom you might want or need, especially during your underclass-man years, while you're still getting your feet under you. (The best jobs, by the way, are in the library. Rarely do you have many responsibilities, and you are surrounded by the wealth of knowledge and seclusion you need to get your work done.)

Typical service jobs, like bartending, waiting tables, and delivering Chinese food, are very difficult to balance with a heavy academic workload. You can make some good money in the service industry, yeah, but you're going to work (and get stressed) for it, and other than some extra coin, you won't really have anything notable to show for your effort. Pour a few drinks; serve some chicken parm; call it a night. And forget labor-intensive jobs like landscaping or construction work. Your schoolwork is already demanding enough of your energy, so there's no need to add more to your plate (unless it has to do with your chosen major). We're trying to be strategic here;

your first—and most important—job is to make grades. (Oh yeah, and be leery of fifteen-dollar-an-hour jobs that tend to be weighted on the commissions you may or may not earn. Advertisements abound on college campuses to MAKE BIG BUCKS NOW.)

So, if you're not going to go the slacker route, where you can get paid to study, you could go a completely different direction and find a job that might actually pay dividends beyond your paycheck. Imagine the benefits if you took on a research role or some other job in academia, where you end up working on a project that you are passionate about. Find a professor who you know is working on a research project and submit the idea to be their assistant (which might mean running for Venti iced mocha latte Frappuccinos—"two creams, three Equals, easy on the foam, please"—and making photocopies, but the idea is that you will be immersed in the academic community). From there, the jump to a more important role is a breeze, and the whole time, as I said, you're building your résumé. "Learn, get paid, and gain valuable experience? Sign me up, Doc." Perhaps, if you do a little planning, this can even coincide with an internship or work-study . . .

Internships and Work-Study

Work-study is designed to allow you to offset the cost of education by trading your sweat and elbow grease for compensation during the college years, rather than merely accepting a check (in the form of a grant or scholarship) for your achievements in high school. The idea is that your college puts you to work as someone's assistant or errand boy for some meager hourly wage, which you can then apply to your astronomical tuition. There are plenty of those aforementioned slacker jobs available as work-study, or as I said before, you might be able to find a situation where you're working in your chosen academic field with a professor and you're able to learn and provide a service and get paid. Either way, take the time to find the most lucrative, best opportunity for you to work on campus.

On-campus work-studies not only cut down on commute time, since you're right there on campus, but they are also a great way to begin to get to know the right people and learn your way around campus. Maybe you get a job working in the cafeteria or with Physical Plant. Great! Imagine the perks of free food or the opportunity to fill your gas tank once a week. Or if you're interested in writing (a very necessary skill to develop!), the school publication might be a perfect fit for you. The more people you meet, the better off you're going to be the next time you're looking for a little good fortune, and work-study gives you the opportunity to meet the right people.

The better work-study opportunities tend to get filled rather quickly, so start looking *right now*. Make phone calls, visit the student employment office, talk to your professors, and get a copy of the school newspaper, but do it now, before you're stuck settling for the last job available (which might be a real job that requires you to actually do work of some kind).

An off-campus internship is different, in several respects, from a work-study or working as a research assistant. The idea is that you get out there in the trenches for a little real-world application of what your professors are throwing at you in the classroom. After all, book smarts are one thing, but actually applying those cognitive skills is the whole point of your education in the first place. By choosing early to merge your work experience with what you're learning in class, you are saying—to yourself and to your prospective employers—that you are serious about your passion for your field of study and you are serious about your future.

Check with your advisor (and maybe even the registrar) to see if there are opportunities available for you to intern during the summer or receive course credit or both. Many students take a semester off from classes to do a full-time internship, and they still graduate in four years. Money, experience, good times, and course credit? *Saaaaaaah-weet.*

For some reason, a lot of my friends never interned during their college years, but the ones who did saw immediate results upon graduation. Not only did they already have a little money banked away and a sturdy résumé, but more important, they had job offers waiting for them as they walked off the stage with their diplomas. There is no question that an internship can give you a leg up against your peers.

Be an RA

Do yourself one favor in college. Okay, three. First, study abroad. We'll talk about that later. Second, get a group of friends together for a home game of a random, less popular, underattended sporting event and cheer like the Sox are playing the Yankees in game 7. I'm saying go nuts. Make signs; paint your faces; bring noisemakers; invent a couple of cheers. It really might be the most fun two-hour stretch of your entire college experience. Third, be an RA for at least one of your upperclassmen years. Being an RA changed my life. And I'm not one to make dramatic empty statements like that.

I basically went to college to play basketball. Without hoops, I don't know what would have happened to me. After high school graduation, I didn't have any scholarship opportunities (and Mommy and Daddy had zero dollars saved for my college education), so I enrolled in the local community college where I started half-assing my way through a few prerequisite courses. A couple opportunities arose for me to play college ball, and I took the one that looked the most promising, at Merrimack.

My freshman year went all right. I struggled to prove myself in the early games, but I started the last six games of the season and even hit seven threes in our final game. I was pumped for a solid college basketball experience. I went home for the summer, hit the gym, and came back with high hopes.

From there, my career nosedived, but I'll save that for another book.

Nearing Christmas break of our sophomore year, my roommate Bruno saw an advertisement to be an RA. I didn't know what kind of responsibilities that entailed, but I knew that it meant a steady paycheck and one grand per semester toward room and board. "Um, you say you want me to sign here and initial here?"

So initially, I was in it for the money and much less interested in the social ramifications of being an RA. Even after I met Donna, the director of residence life, and she began to explain something about "making a difference in your residents' lives," I wasn't really that interested. "Where can we pick up our paychecks?"

See, when I began college, it was never my intention to do anything other than toss an inflated leather ball through an iron ring, but then I became an RA and I began to see things from a whole different angle. I began to see what being an RA was all about. I became more involved around campus than I ever imagined was possible. I began to appreciate social and political issues. I was responsible for a group of twenty-four young'n's on my floor, who were constantly coming to me with the most preposterous issues that you could ever imagine. I was invited to speak all over campus. I volunteered. I brought *The Amazing Race* to the Merrimack campus. Blah, blah, blah. I did, I did, I did. Three cheers for me. Point is, I got involved and I had fun. (And again, I got paid for it.)

So I'm not kidding when I say that being an RA changed my life. I loved it. I built a foundation of leadership skills that have helped me become the person I am today. Without those two great years, I would have been just another washed-up athlete running around campus with my head down, wondering what happened to his proposed illustrious career. Instead, I was a washed-up athlete who padded his résumé, got paid, and perhaps, most important, met some of the most fascinating, ambitious students on campus. It really was the best opportunity that I took advantage of during college.

Most schools have even better packages than the one offered at Merrimack. You might be able to get a free meal plan or a free room. When you're a freshman, find out what being an RA is all about at your school. Talk with the RAs and the hall director in your dorm. Go meet the director of residence life and tell them who you are and what you're all about. (Chapter 8 of *Scratch Beginnings* will get you the job, *guaranteed*.) Stick your foot in the door now, and the application process will be that much easier when the time comes. (Because it is such a rewarding *and* demanding job, being an RA is one job you will most definitely have to fight—tooth and nail—to get.)

Foster Your Inner Entrepreneur

If there's a great opportunity to get in touch with the entrepreneur within, college is it, for sure. After all, you have a campus full of ideal clientele—people who trust you and whose needs and wants you are associated with (and can therefore satisfy). Of course, there's the argument that college kids are broke, but they always seem to have an extra ten or fifteen dollars lying around to spend on a T-shirt that you design or any of a host of services that you can conjure up.

I sold T-shirts on campus, and then I took my venture to the streets of Boston, where I earned plenty of extra spending money after Red Sox games. Really. Drunk Red Sox fans will buy anything, especially after a win, and the ugly T-shirts I had for sale were a testament to that. Passersby screamed nightly, "Did you design that shirt yourself on Word? I wouldn't use that shirt as an oil rag!" Ah, my memories of the streets around Fenway. I had a lot of fun, I met some cool people, and I saw more than my fair share of after-hours activities.

My friend Dave Dlugasch started a business where he (and his cousin) designed customized buddy icons for Instant Messenger. They didn't make a fortune, but they built the business, made a little money, and then sold it for double their start-up investment. Not a bad way to spend your idle hours in college: earn money, meet valuable contacts, and learn a lesson or two.

You might want to check the legalities of doing business on your campus before you purchase a mass quantity of something and start knocking on doors to sell it. All the kids that sold shirts—or whatever—on Merrimack's campus were breaking the rules, but nobody got caught and most of them paid for their spring-break trips in just a few nights. Risky, but potentially worth it in the end.

Build Your Network

They say it's not what you know but rather who you know that is more important to your success in life. I've even heard it mentioned that the true value of an Ivy League diploma, for example, isn't as much about the actual level of education you obtain, but more about the fact that you spend four years hobnobbing with the big boys. I think you need a balance of specialized skills to go along with your network, but at least to a point, there is truth to knowing the right people on your way to the top, and here's your chance to prove that. This is why the jobs you take in college could pay huge dividends down the road.

No matter which direction you're headed by working in college, start building your network now—through the career center, the alumni office, professional organizations, faculty. If you take the time to please them, they will be more than happy to return the favor down the road. (We'll delve deeper into this issue in chapter 10: Get Connected, Stay Connected.)

Cash Is King

You're going to spend money in college. Lots of it. And not just on tuition, room, board, books, and booze. One curious aspect about college is that there's always another expense waiting for you when you just happened to spend your last few dollars. You just made a Wal-Mart run, and your phone bill just came in the mail. You saved for two weeks to take your girlfriend out for a lovely evening, and now there's a once-in-a-lifetime rafting trip to West Virginia, and you don't want to be the only one left out. And then your car needs an oil change, and you need to go to the doctor for a checkup, and on and on. There's always something.

Sticking to a tight budget in college is tricky (but doable), and the secret is getting into the right mind-set, establishing needs versus wants, and so on. I imagine you're already on your way there, since it is universal knowledge that you'll never be as broke as you are in college, so let's see what you can do to make the most of your new life of poverty.

Pay Cash (or Use Your Debit Card) Whenever Possible

You won't have to worry at all about going into debt. Got it? Good. Moving on . . . .

Get a Checking Account

First things first. Get a checking account. Solicit a few banks in the area of your college and find the best deal. Most banks, especially those close to your school, will have special deals available for students. Depending on how much you research the opportunities out there, you might be able to find a bank that offers no monthly fees ("When you open an account with us *right now!*") or special rates or a teddy bear for signing up. More than likely, you're going to be bombarded on opening weekend with plenty of opportunities to get signed up. The banks will come courting right when you arrive on campus. Aren't they nice?

There are other factors that you'll also want to consider. Is the bank local, or does it have branches (and ATMs) nationwide that make traveling a lot more convenient? A lot of places won't accept out-of-state checks. What kinds of fees are associated with online checking or bouncing a check (which totally never happens) or visiting the ATM? Are they crazy busy and understaffed, or will they have time to sit down and talk to you about your personal financial situation should an issue arise?

What is their customer service like in the first place? Does each teller have a basket of lollipops in front of them?

You are big business for a bank, and don't forget that. Right now, your balance is in the double or triple digits, but they want to serve you now so they can have your business later when your balance moves to the right a couple decimal points. So if they don't seem like they want to work with you, move on. The next bank will be ready with an application.

> Also, be diligent about balancing your checkbook. Even if you are following your ledger online, keep an eye on every transaction with your debit card, every check you write, every deposit you make, and every online transfer Daddy makes into your account. Since your account will be near zero quite frequently while you're in college, one slipup can cost you an exorbitant fee for overdrawing.

Life's a Budget

The idea of budgeting is actually kind of simple: income must be greater than expenses. You don't need to study economics to understand that. But budgeting is much more difficult since your income is low—damn low—and people keep trying to take your dollars from you.

The manner in which you establish a budget can be as simple or complex as your spending habits require. If you live a pretty simple life, you might not have to write anything down at all— you can just crunch a few numbers in your head about where you need to be allocating your resources. But if your life is more complex (maybe you have a truly meager fixed income and outrageous expenses), you will want to sit down and start breaking down the financial figures of your life. Start with your monthly income and then list your expenses in order of priority. Your phone bill; laundry, food, and transportation expenses; and a monthly allotment for toiletries all might be high on the list. Do a few calculations to see what you have left to work with after that, and that will give you a better idea how much money you can spend each month (and week and day) on groceries and concerts. The *worst* is getting to the end of the month with an empty purse in your left hand and a bill in your right. Then you've got to suck up your pride and call somebody for help. Bad news. Prepare a budget now, and that won't happen.

Surely you've already mapped out the value stores close to school, but also understand that there are discounts being offered all over town for students. Everywhere. From the movies to the local drugstore to *all* area restaurants, businesses want to get their grubby hands on your wallet, so have your student ID handy and seek out the best deals around town before you start spending your hard-earned money.

Needs Versus Wants

Just as you schedule a balance between your needs and your wants, you have to do the same with your finances. YOU HAVE TO!! I'm yelling at you with an extra exclamation point because I know what you're thinking: "Geez, Shep. I get it. Needs versus wants. Blah, blah. How old do you think I am? I'm grown, and I'm not a dummy." Right, but at the same time, there is a fine line of needs versus wants to tread in college that didn't exist before. In high school, food was food. No questions asked. Now, food in the cafeteria is not the same as food ordered out (in taste or cost), and food ordered out is not the same as going out to eat. The difference might be a few dollars, but those few dollars multiplied over the course of a semester can add up and come back to hammer you. Do you *need* to eat out with such frequency or do you *want* to? (By the way, that late-night fourth meal alone can kill your fiscal situation and really give you a head start on the Freshman Fifteen.)

And it's not just food. Take the time to appreciate the value in saving a few dollars on everything from clothes to school supplies to entertainment. There is *so much* free entertainment to be had in college ("free" = the hefty "Student Activities Fee" that you already paid) that you shouldn't even budget for entertainment (unless ordering a round of buffalo wings and watching *City of God* by yourself on Friday night is your idea of entertainment, in which case, you need to forget all of this money business and skip immediately with your highlighter to chapter 8). Well, okay, maybe a few dollars, but don't go nuts scheduling (and paying for) off-campus activities when there's so much to discover right there in your college community, no matter how big or small it is.

Deciphering between needs and wants is more of a challenge than you think. Do you need an iPod or an electric scooter? Of course not. But you also don't need to wear underwear, and you don't need one of your kidneys. They're there for convenience, and they serve a valid purpose. Just be smart and be mindful of your obligation to make a few sacrifices on your way through these next four years. Always consider the cost of something versus the use you will get out of it. Is it worth it?

Don't Buy a Game System

Someone on your floor has one, so go make friends with them, and let them bear the expense. (In my house growing up, this was the swimming pool rule. When I asked if we could build a swimming pool in the backyard, Ma said, "Why do we need a swimming pool? The Richardsons have one. Go make friends with them.")

That said, abusing your leisure time by playing video games can ruin your college experience (and probably your libido). Have fun, but don't glue yourself to the TV.

Big-Ticket Items

If you're spending your money on big-ticket items throughout your four years, then you are trading out—well, your lifestyle. One iPod = 904 bricks of Ramen. One 48" HDTV = 46.4 (good) concert tickets. One electric scooter = seventeen non-electric scooters.

Instead, wait for a gift-giving holiday, like your birthday or Christmas or Martin Luther King Day, and prepare to cash in. Tell your parents to stop buying you all those usual knick-knacks. No more stocking stuffers for you. No sir. You're going for the big time here. Tell them you want a stereo or a TV or something extravagant for your room. Get serious with your parents. That's right; be spoiled. "I'll take one of those, and see if they have it available in a hot magenta, please." College gives you a four-year pass to receive top-notch gifts and, better yet, the right to give cheap homemade gifts to your relatives. "Aw, look honey. Mike sketched us a family portrait. Again." Milk these next four years for all they're worth.

Master negotiators can take this tactic to the next level by requesting super-duper big-ticket items and then "settling" for lesser items. "Okay, Pops, check this out. I really would like the BMW 335d for Christmas, which is actually an older model than I'd prefer, but whatever. I'm willing to settle, just this one Christmas, for a 46" BRAVIA® Z Series LCD flat-panel HDTV with Motionflow™ 120Hz and the Advanced Contrast Enhancer circuit. Here's a picture, here are the stores in the area where it's available, and here are directions to each of those stores. Great. Well, I'm gonna go for a jog. Nice talk, Pops." He might roll his eyes, but check under the tree on December 25. I'll bet there's a 46" BRAVIA® Z Series waiting for you.

> Request big-ticket items as gifts, and spend your hard-earned, paltry paycheck on smaller items and activities throughout the semester.

Travel

As the months pass, you're going to learn the different ways you can cut corners and save money in college. Buying textbooks is one of those areas (buy used, borrow new, but get only what you need). Transportation is another.

If you live far from college—or even if you don't—it can cost you big bucks to commute back and forth on breaks. This is the perfect time to get creative. Check with airlines or a travel agent to see what kind of deals they can offer you. Get a frequent-flier card now! Even if you use it only once or twice a year, those miles add up. Read the paper for travel deals. Get to know people from nearby your town so that you can have a commuting buddy or buddies—for conversation and economy—rather than footing the entire bill to travel solo. Actually, if you can, avoid having a car with you at college altogether. (Revert to Ma's swimming pool rule, above.) Having a car will be expensive, no doubt about that, and it could be more troublesome than you can imagine, especially since you'll become the transportation for all of your friends for off-campus social events.

Credit Crunch

Oh, dear reader. If only I could turn back the hands of time! Few people have made the mistakes in their financial lives that I have. Truly. I turned a hot stock tip into three years of misery complete with $17,224.83(!) in interest payments. What a disaster that was. It really put a damper on an otherwise-prosperous college career.

So, it happens. Mistakes happen, period, and that includes credit mistakes. Fair enough. But don't use that as a cop-out or an excuse to set yourself back two, five, ten years, or more when you could instead set yourself up to flourish. Some people have been in debt their entire lives, and it stemmed from the fiscal foundation they established for themselves while they were in college. This, your first shot at independence of any kind, is a perfect opportunity to heed a valuable lesson or two (before you're taught a valuable lesson or two).

Build Credit Responsibly

Getting a credit card is easy. Piece of cake. I got one when I was sixteen years old. The credit card company didn't know I was sixteen, nor did it care. I was paying interest, and that's all that interested them. (Hahahaha! Get it? *Interested* them. Oh, man. That was a good one. Oh, man. Whew.) But seriously, Visa, MasterCard, American Express, and Discover are fighting for your business, just like any other company. They love you, and they don't even know you. You're a huge credit risk to them, and that's why you're so appealing: the more you default and the later you pay, the more your rates and penalty charges go up and the more money they make. *Cha-ching!* They *hope* you don't pay on time. After all, they are going to get their money, somehow, guaranteed. Trust me.

So, the first lesson is to be careful. Credit card companies are going to throw all kinds of T-shirts or NERF Footballs or financial incentives your way just to get you to sign up. Don't be a sucker. Really, you don't even need a credit card in the first place (other than perhaps for an emergency, but even then, hopefully, you have enough money on your debit card to suffice), but you definitely shouldn't have a credit card if you're the kind of person who just likes to go to the mall to "look around" or "see what's on sale." I'll tell you what's on sale at the mall: nothing. It was overpriced in the first place, and now you're just paying a reduction from those high prices. And fast-food joints. If you're putting fast-food purchases on your credit card, you, my friend, are going to go broke very quickly. A stack of credit cards can be poison in your pants, especially when the bills start to roll in and you see that you're actually paying for that initial "free" gift in the form of an annual fee or interest.

A few tips on building credit:

1. Don't charge more than you can afford to pay every month.
2. Pay your *entire* balance on time, every time. You'll avoid paying any interest at all and you won't have to worry about digging yourself into debt. Paying your balance right away is the best method of building credit responsibly.

3. Get a card without an annual fee. There are so many competing credit card companies out there that you shouldn't have to pay for these services.
4. Weigh the benefits of each credit card that you're looking at. You can earn all kinds of miles or points for every dollar you spend.
5. Use your card only for emergencies or needs. Pay cash (or use your debit card) for your wants.
6. Write CHECK ID in the space requesting your signature on the back. Better yet, get a card with your mug shot on the front. Identity theft is a growing epidemic in this country, and every victim "never thought it would happen to little old me." Well, it did, and now it's going to take years and lots of phone calls to get it all squared away.

Five-Hundred-Dollar Limit

Really, what are you going to buy that costs more than five hundred dollars with your credit card? As I said, credit is for *emergencies*; pay cash for everything else. If you really, truly want something now, you'll still really, truly want it by the time you take a couple of weeks to save up for it.

If a credit card company offers to raise your credit limit, you tell them, "No thanks, but . . . uh . . . if you'd like to lower my interest rate, that would be nice." Once you've started to build your reputation as a responsible, bill-paying member of society, you will have the leeway to negotiate with these companies. "Y'know, Big Billy Bob's Bank is offering me 9.2 percent interest, but you're charging me 13.9 percent. Whatd'ya say we lower mine a couple points, or should I just head on over there to Big Billy Bob?" Seriously, call them (every six months). They'll jump through fire to retain you as their customer.

Mind Your Credit Report, Mind Your Taxes

If you have read this far and are still considering using a credit card (to build your credit responsibly!), then make sure you keep an eye on your credit report. No one can be certain how it's calculated—it's kind of like the recipe for Coke—but you can be certain that when it's time for you to fill out an application for an apartment or car loan, apply for a mortgage, or even apply for a job, your credit rating matters.

You can request your free credit report, once a year, from AnnualCreditReport.com.

Use only this site. Plenty of imposters out there would love for you to get sucked into their "free credit reporting," and then sign you up for plenty of other "free services" once you give them your credit card information.

Also, there are tax advantages to working as a student, but you still need to keep a close eye on what taxes are being taken out of your check. Maybe next April 15 you'll be receiving a refund, or maybe you'll need to be prepared for the IRS to stick you with a tax bill.

Be on a First-Name Basis With Your Financial-Aid Advisor

I could spend pages and pages talking about the different ways to fund your education and all the fantastic scholarship and grant opportunities available to a strapping young student like yourself. Indeed, there's an entire section at Barnes & Noble filled with books on financing the most debt-ridden period of your life, but there's not a whole lot of sense in me just skimming the surface here. It would be a waste of time for both of us.

There is some great advice I can offer you, though, and that is to be on a first-name basis with your financial-aid advisor.

Before you even get to school, get them on the phone or meet with them in their office. When you arrive on campus, go meet them. After a couple of months, go touch base, just to see what they're doing. "Hey, just thought I'd stop by to say hi. How's your daughter doing?" Take a box of chocolates with you. I'm not kidding! Unless you're on full scholarship already (and actually, even if you are on full scholarship), your financial-aid advisor is going to be your best friend while you're in school. Seriously. Why? Because the financial-aid advisor at your school knows where to get money to pay for college and they know how to do it. They have the resources in their office and they know which direction to point you for additional opportunities (like Fastweb.com). The more they know about you and your personal circumstances (financial situation, academic record, hobbies, talents, interests, whether your parents are still married or you were raised by a single working mom), the better they can help you. And they will. A lot of people on your campus might see you as a nuisance if you come fishing for assistance, but there's something about financial-aid advisors getting excited (genuinely excited) about helping you that you might not find from other people around campus.

Think about it. If you invest all this time with your financial-aid advisor and they're only able to scrounge up a measly extra thousand dollars for you, wouldn't you say even that's worth it?

Oh yeah, that reminds me. Make sure you fill out at least eight to twelve scholarship applications per school year. Eight to twelve! Do it. *Apply early. Apply often.* That's your motto when hunting for dough for college. You'll be so grateful you did. Think about your time versus your money. If you take a couple of Saturday afternoons and spend ten hours filling out ten applications and you get only one silly little thousand-dollar scholarship, you just made a hundred dollars an hour. Which is about fourteen times what you're getting paid at the copy shop. And which is about six times what you're going to get paid once you have your diploma. And which is just one more accomplishment you can add to your already-bulky résumé. Stop me if I'm going too fast here.

Even if you already get plenty of money in the form of scholarships or grants or the fund that your parents set up for you when you were born, you can still get more. There are all kinds of free money out there. The upside is unlimited here. They don't put a cap on it. The less you have to pay back after college, the more freedom you will have with your first five years out of college (down payment on a house, anyone?). I know people who actually got paid to go to college (you're talking to one right here). I just kept applying for scholarships and grants from private organizations or the government or whoever wanted to give them to me, and I ended up banking about $2,200 per semester. Literally. My girlfriend was going to bitch to the bursar's office about "all of these ridiculous fees," and I was stopping by at the beginning of the semester to pick up a check. I thank you kindly.

And then I spent it all on a hot penny stock that went under.

Graduating With Debt

If you graduate without debt, then you are most absolutely a member of the minority. That's like walking through the mall and not buying anything. It happens, but rarely. Most students take out loans to pay their tuition or have to use a credit card during their college days in order to pay for food, books, and other basic school supplies. No worries. It happens.

It's important to maintain the same spending habits you had during college for at least a couple years after college. Once you receive that first considerable paycheck, start making payments toward your loans (even if you are allowed to wait until six months after graduation). Don't go crazy with a new car or new gadgets until you've begun to make a considerable whack at your student loans. You'll hate it at first, but you'll thank yourself in five years when your friends are still paying down their student loans and you're able to buy a boat or move forward with a down payment on a house or pay cash for extended vacations.

> Even if you're debt-free upon graduation, maintaining the same college spending habits for a few years can pay heavy dividends for you down the line. Invest your extra dollars rather than spending them on things you don't really need. Feed your mutual fund, buy an investment property, maximize your retirement account, or whatever. Just put those early extra dollars to work for you now. Graduating debt-free is a gift that a lot of students don't have, so use this opportunity rather than squandering it.

Chapter in Brief

Okey dokey, let's review:

- Rather than spending your time waiting tables or bartending (which could earn a good paycheck), take on a worthy internship or work-study where you can make money and pad your résumé.
- Be an RA at least one year during your college career.

- Have a budget and pay that budget with cash. Establish needs versus wants. Be mindful of the money you're spending for big-ticket items and travel.
- Your credit future is your responsibility now. Be responsible. A thousand-dollar credit limit is plenty, and pay down your balance *in full* every month.
- Establish a rapport with your financial-aid advisor.

FOUR

Be an Expert

Your first priority in college—*above all else*—is to get an education. It's important to get involved and meet great people and take this opportunity to really get to know who you are on the inside. All these are skills and experiences that you will carry forward with you the rest of your life, but the bottom line is you are here to develop your knowledge and skills beyond the level of those who—well, aren't going to college. If you drink and party and sleep your way through college, you're going to fail, you're going to waste tons of time and money, and you're going to look back at the last four years thinking, "Gosh darn it. I could've done so much more."

Before we get into discussing some seriously useful study tips (in the next chapter), let's pause for a few pages and consider your motive for coming to college in the first place. You're here to find your passion (I hope), but that's easier conceived than done, especially if you spend the next four years spreading yourself too thin by trying to get involved in everything.

Specialize in Something

If you tore a ligament in your ankle, would you rather have an obstetrician operate on you or a foot specialist? Would you rather an attorney do your taxes or a CPA? And would you rather watch a highlight film of average skiers going down a mountain or guys who have dedicated their lives to learning flips and twists?

Take a second to think back in history to the greats— anybody who would be considered the best at what they do. When I say "author" or "speaker" or "president" or "fashion designer" or "kung fu master," there are names that immediately come to mind. In fields of science or mathematics or engineering, you might be acquainted with the names of specialized experts who aren't celebrities but have still made incredible advancements in their fields. Why are they great? Simply put, they took the time to sharpen their skills to become the best they could possibly be at their chosen occupations. They became the best at one thing. From there, some branch out to achieve greatness elsewhere, perhaps, but the point is that they started in one area.

College is a unique experience in that you have the opportunity to spend your time: A.) goofing off; B.) learning a little bit about a bunch of things; or C.) really developing a specialized skill in one area. It is very easy to get lost—on a small or a large campus—if you fail to understand the idea that you are here to accelerate your savvy in a specific field.

Be #1 at One Thing

Think about it. Imagine you are the chief executive of a company and sitting across the desk from you is yet another fresh college graduate hoping to wow you to the point that you'll hire them for a permanent position. When you ask the question, Why should I hire you?, are you going to be more impressed by somebody who starts kicking out a long-winded, complex answer about all their talents and abilities, or do you want someone who sits back in their chair, crosses their right leg over their left, and confidently (not arrogantly) proclaims, "Well, Ms. CEO, I'll tell ya. I love electrical engineering. It's my passion. But more than that, the fact is that I'm the best electrical engineer you're going to find. I've spent the last four years of my life learning everything I can possibly learn about this trade, and I'm excited to take my expertise to the next level by working for you. I can type seventy-eight words per minute, and I'm quite proficient at math, but a lot of your applicants have those abilities. None of your applicants, though, are the best electrical engineer you're going to find. I am."

If you don't know the answer as to which one a CEO will choose, I'll tell you. A CEO is going to hire the person who gives the second answer. Why? Listen—a firm can find somebody (anybody!) who's pretty good at a bunch of things. It's not that hard to do, really, because plenty of people are graduating from America's universities with loads of mediocre talent in a variety of areas. But few are graduating with the specialized capabilities to outshine their fellow graduates. This is fascinating, ironic even, because companies (especially in today's global economy) are looking for specialists. They can send secondary tasks overseas to India, but they need people domestically that can do what no one else around can do. So, if you can sit back in your chair, cross your legs, and determine that you have spent the last four years of college becoming the best, you are a much more marketable candidate than the next guy who has spread his talent and resources too thin. You want to be known in your field. "Web design? You should go see Maribel. Nobody does web design like her."

By the way, this is an opportune time to really use that internship—as I mentioned before—to your advantage. If you can walk off the college campus with that real-world experience already under your belt, you are clearly making the right strides to becoming an authority in your industry.

It is also important to extend this idea beyond the realm of academia and really kick-start your social life. You're already working to be the best accountant in the history of the modern world, and now you can put in the work to master the guitar, or be the most eloquent poet on campus, or be the person that everybody wants to pick for their intramural soccer team. Not only will you develop the self-assurance that you are great at something, but your peers will begin to recognize that, as well, and you won't have to run around campus telling everybody to "stop a second and listen to this great poem I wrote. Y'know, 'cuz I'm a great poet." Creating an identity by mastering a talent (that you love!) bumps you ahead of your peers who are perhaps being reckless with their idle hours.

Read the Newspaper Every Morning

While you're branding yourself to be the best in your field, it is still important to have a wide perspective on the world around you. It's imperative that you know what's going on, that you try to stay on top of current events, even if it's just a broad overview. You don't want to be that person who has to always hear about it from the next guy. You want to be worldly and cultured and abreast of what's hip, and reading the newspaper every day can do that for you. I learned this lesson early, when I would sit silently (and unaware) around the lunch table while everybody else debated mainstream issues. And I'm not one to remain silent. It's hard to put a lid on me, but if I didn't know what was going on, what was there for me to say?

Reading the newspaper, though, which could otherwise be a daunting task, doesn't involve sitting down at the breakfast table, inhaling your eggs and bacon, and then slowly digesting each line of each page of the newspaper. Shoot, you'll still be sitting there at lunchtime. Who reads the whole paper, anyway? Read what interests you or what appears to be important, and skim the rest. Newspaper editors do the work for you by putting the more pertinent issues on the front pages of each section, so breeze through those stories and then move through the other sections. Get the gist of the civil wars and famine and other world events. Read about the local heroes, statewide drought issues, and the nationwide political controversies. Find out who won Wimbledon and read why the state's football team can't seem to get it together despite preseason predictions that had them atop the national polls. And what does the local arts scene look like this week?

A lot of colleges offer free copies of the local or state paper, or even *USA Today*. If you can get your hands on a copy of the in-depth reporting of the *New York Times*, that would be gold. You might like the *Wall Street Journal*, but that newspaper has always been too overwhelming for unsophisticated people like me. Or you can get whatever news you want online (for free) if that's more convenient. Doesn't really matter; just exercise your brain by getting your eyes on the news.

> You can read through the entire newspaper in ten to twenty minutes, and it might be the best ten to twenty minutes you spend all day.

Choosing a Major

Taking the initial leap to college might be the easy part if you consider the pressures of what you have to actually accomplish while you're there, not the least of which is deciding what you're going to do for the rest of your life after college. Perhaps you're already in touch with your life's passion and know exactly what your area of study is going to be, or maybe part of your reasoning for going to college in the first place is to find out what it is that you really want to do. Whatever your motive, choosing a major is a vital step in ensuring that you don't spend the next four years building a faulty foundation for the next forty.

Work on Core Requirements While Deciding What Your Major Will Be

If you have no idea where your life is headed, that's fine. Well, to a certain degree. Just because you "don't know" doesn't mean you should delay important life decisions (like declaring your major) by being lazy—as in, "Eh . . . well, I'll just wait until next semester to decide what I'd like to study." Not knowing is one thing. Delaying the decision-making process is another.

While you're exploring what you'd like to study, you can bulk up on core requirements, which you then won't have to worry about later. Every college has this set of classes that you must complete before you can receive your diploma. In fact, a large chunk of the courses you take will be nonmajor required courses anyway. Core requirements vary from college to college, so make sure you have a clear picture before your first day of classes. Some schools might require introductions to the sciences as part of your core curriculum, while others may put more focus on the humanities. Most colleges have course requirements in nearly every area of study. Find out what the situation is at your school. Then, sift through the course catalogue and start making a "to take" list of the courses you might be interested in. If you've already declared your major, you can balance your major requirements with core requirements by rationing out your classes over four years. On the other hand, if you don't know what you're going to study, you can spend your first two or three semesters completing your core requirements, and then you'll have the freedom to focus on your major in your sophomore year. (Some colleges have this set up for you already by not even allowing you to declare your major until your sophomore or junior year.)

Decide What You Like

Let's be honest. There are people who have it all planned out. They charted the road maps of their lives when they were twelve, and they've been following those road maps ever since. "I'll go to college and study molecular biology and then take a year off to travel before I get my master's degree and get married at twenty-eight (in the summer in New Hampshire, or in the South in the spring because I want an outdoor wedding that isn't too hot) and, at thirty, have two children, which I'll conceive in October because I don't want their birthdays to be too close to a major holiday, and . . ." And here you are, thinking, "Well . . . uh . . . . I'm not quite sure I know what I want to do." No worries! Just because you spend your freshman year with an undeclared major while your friends are diving headfirst into their chosen fields of study doesn't mean you're behind. It just means you're being patient with this decision-making process. Cool. But you can still learn what you would like to do. Continue to explore your interests. Get involved with different projects and organizations around campus to see what piques your curiosity. The decision on what you're destined to study is *not* going to simply appear one day. You have to go out and find it.

Use your core requisite classes as an opportunity to see what you might be interested in. You may never discover your passion for philosophy if you don't ever take a course to find out what it's all about. Another promising tactic for discovering what you'd like to declare as your major is to seek advice from those around you (beyond your friends and family, who may tend to be a little biased). Go to your academic advisor or look up a couple professors in fields of study that you're considering and ask to meet with them for five minutes. You can sit in on a class or (if you say, "please") maybe even get your hands dirty for a day or two on an activity they're working on. Professors will be happy to explain and answer your questions, as they are always recruiting prospects for their field. Don't get in anybody's way, but it's important that you really *know* what you want to do before you dive in. Really. I have several friends who are going back to school now, at thirty years old, because they really wanted to be nurses but they studied finance instead.

Ah, that reminds me of another mistake that you want to avoid. *Do not choose your major based on how much money you can possibly make in that industry.* Ugh, what a mistake that is. People think that they can study law or medicine or finance and they'll make bundles of money. Which is true. But do you love law or medicine or finance? Are you willing to spend your life dedicated to that profession? Are you willing

and prepared to put in the extra years of study—and added
expense—to become a doctor or a lawyer or an investment
banker? Love what you study; don't choose a major because
it has the greatest fiscal reward or because your parents told
you that you'd "always be able to find a job if you just studied
what I studied."

That being said, there is a really powerful government-
sponsored Internet resource called the *Occupational Outlook
Handbook* (BLS.gov/oco), which introduces jobs that would
never occur to people (and those that you're already considering). It is a great resource for evaluating the differences between occupations—job environment, pace of the day, outlook
for a particular field, required education, how competitive it is,
growth potential, et cetera.

If you pick a major and decide your heart's not in it, change
it. It's not that difficult to do. Don't "push it out" because you're
already so far in. A few wasted credit hours are easier to handle
than wasted years down the line. My college roommate Lightfoot changed his major three times before he was set on what
he wanted to study.

Take Astronomy or Art History

You can't be a robot. You can't be just an electrical engineer.
Professional schools and employers (more today than ever
before) love an applicant with diverse interests and knowledge.
(And here I've spent this whole chapter telling you to be an
expert at one thing. Am I contradicting myself here or what?)
You do, indeed, need to be great at one thing. Distinguish
yourself from your peers. Be the best, and you're hired after

college. All true. College, though, is also your chance to begin to branch out and really get educated about the world around you. Reading the newspaper every day is a great start. Studying abroad will be a fantastic opportunity for you. Watching foreign films without the subtitles is classy and broadens your horizons. You can be great at one thing first and then really expand your knowledge beyond that one thing to become a well-rounded individual.

If you're already required to take certain courses anyway, why not take a course or two that you've always been curious about but never had the time or resources to delve into? You can learn to rock climb or play an instrument or cook food from around the world. Take an acting or speech class so you can develop your command of the English language. You can take an art-history course or an astronomy course. How cool is it to stand on the back deck of a cocktail party, look up at the stars, and point out the different constellations to your lovely companion (when she otherwise might have ditched you for being stale just like everybody else at the party)? And when you travel to Italy or France or New York and go to all of these cool art museums, you can be the person that says, "Oh, you guys don't know about this one? Let me tell you a little som'n' som'n'." Personally, I know if I could go back and do it all over again, I would have taken some kind of dancing course (any kind of dancing course!). Now I have to play catch-up with my uncoordinated feet, and I have to pay for these classes without a student discount.

While I was in college, I chose to focus on a foreign language. I was not only passionate about studying Spanish, but I also saw it as a very pragmatic skill in today's world (especially to go along with my business degree). As it turns out, English is the language of business in the world, but it isn't the only spoken or written language (or even the most dominant), so it might help to broaden your perspective by picking up a second language. Besides, it's fun to speak with the natives when you go abroad. My goodness, ladies dig a guy who can speak in a foreign tongue. (Yes, you do! Don't lie.) Or know how to dance. Listen to me. If you can learn to dance or play an instrument or pick up a foreign language in college, you will be dating out of your league for the rest of your life. And vice versa for the ladies. Just make sure you carry an interest in the extracurricular courses that you choose or you'll end up spending the semester in gloom, which will be a waste of money for you and a waste of time for your professor.

Don't discount the value that a minor (or even a second major) can have on building your résumé, especially if you can put two pertinent fields of study together (as I did with business and Spanish). That secondary area of study can complement you being the best at something else.

Writing

You might think this is the part of the book where I hop on my soapbox and spit out words of wisdom from a clearly biased perspective. "I'm a writer! You be one, too!" But that's not the angle I'm taking here. The fact is I never wanted to be a writer. I've written my ideas down in journals for the last ten or so years of my life, and I've always taken English courses seriously (and I love to read), but I never aspired to write a book one day, as so many other people do. My teachers told me writing was a necessary skill, so I stuck with it.

And boy, am I glad I did.

You don't have to major in English or be a scientific researcher destined to write grants for the rest of your life before you make the decision to develop your writing. Why? Quite simply, you need to be a good writer, no matter what direction you head in life. If you want to see your résumé filtered to the bottom of the pile, try e-mailing "GR8" or "LOL" to a prospective employer after you graduate. I can't tell you how frustrating it is for me to get e-mails from "educated" people—executives, parents, my own friends—who struggle to form complete sentences, don't punctuate correctly, or can't distinguish between "your" and "you're" or "their," "they're," and "there." It's sad and it's frustrating, and it undermines otherwise-strong ideas. The trouble is that we've developed a culture that thinks only a select group of people need to be strong at composing prose and that if we choose particular majors or occupations, we won't need to be able to write. This is patently false. No matter who you are or what you decide to do, you're going to write for the rest of your life, so you need to learn how to do it well. Failing to develop the proper skills now will create bad habits and problems later.

Write Outside of Class

You're going to write in every class. The exception might be math, but that's about it. In all your other courses, you'll be required to write, whether it's a reflection paper or test answers in essay form or passing notes to your neighbor about the fact that your professor continues to wear that BOOKS HAVE FEELINGS, TOO sweatshirt. Which is good. This will help you sharpen your writing. But it's not enough.

Assign yourself time outside of class to write. Maybe it's ten minutes a day in the morning or an hour at night. The extent to which you decide to write doesn't matter. Just do it. Take out a pad and pen or sit down at your computer (unplug the Internet!) and start writing. A paragraph, a page. *It doesn't matter!* Write what you did that day or what you ate or what's going on in the world, and your reflections on it. Dig deep. "I had chicken and peas for dinner and I met a cute boy named Dave" is not going to suffice. Bust out a thesaurus, and throw a couple of complex sentences in there. Get excited with some exclamation points!!!! "And quotations." Àňð ƒůňķ¥ $¥ᴍßϴℓ$. The best part of all is that writing is therapeutic. I'm telling you. There are times when I'm fuming, leave-me-the-hell-alone mad, and I'll sit down to write out my thoughts, and fifteen minutes later I'm reconstructed. Truly. I'm not kidding when I say writing could save your college career. The most entertaining part is that today, when I look back at what I've written over the years and what an idiot I was, I can't believe I wanted to marry Rachel Bromelas when I was fourteen. Now she has three kids with three different dudes. *Whew.* Dodged a bullet on that one. Also, making a habit of writing will not only improve your skills as a writer but will mark who you were at different points in your life.

I have two friends that—get this—wrote books in college! They weren't gifted writers or authors before they matriculated (one ended up being a poli-sci major, and the other studied engineering), but they wrote books while they were in college. Imagine that. They sat back and did a little math: "Okay, I've got a pretty solid idea here. If I write just two hundred fifty words per day for just a hundred fifty days per year . . . over four years that will be . . . *a friggin' book!*" So, they started writing, and four years later, they bound their manuscripts into book form. Their books are terrible, but *they wrote books*, and that is what matters.

I'm not saying you have to write a book. I'm just saying that e-mails and Facebook messages don't count. Neither does texting. Writing for your school newspaper does, though. So does blogging. A lot of people who never really cared to write before have started blogs while in college—just because they had something to say and they needed a forum in which to say it—and now, all of a sudden, their sites have blown up, and they have people subscribing to their blogs, and they're selling advertisements. You don't have to take it to that level if you don't want to, but again, blogging is a good way to polish your writing and voice your points of view. (It also takes quite a commitment, by the way, depending on how serious you are about it. If you think you spend too much time on the computer already, stay away from the "Oh, I can't wait to get back to my room to post about this" world of blogging.)

Write Well

The whole idea behind additional writing exercises is improvement. Get better every time you write. Build your vocabulary; understand sentence structure; break a paragraph off at the right moment and start a new one; be loose with your form—as if you're having a conversation with the paper or keypad—and then go back and tighten it up. Writing is one thing, but writing well is another. You want to look back at your writing from a month ago and scoff at how terrible it is. All those lessons you learned from your high school English teacher? It's not your professor's job to teach them to you all over again. They're going to put a letter grade at the top of your paper and send you off to someone else to explain why you got that grade. They don't have the time or the patience to stress over your poor composition. If you don't have the luxury of having someone like the editor at the school newspaper critiquing your work, go to the writing center and get a tutor. Now! Heck, you're paying for these services with your tuition dollars anyway, so you might as well use them, right?

If you want to succeed in college and beyond, you have to write and you have to write well, so master it in and out of the classroom. Now, I'm not a great writer by any means. That last page alone, I have two run-on sentences and a paragraph's worth of sentence fragments. Editors love taking a red pen to my manuscripts. But I *wrote this book* because I've worked to add writing to my skill set over the years.

Chapter in Brief

Okey dokey, let's review:

- Be number one at one thing, and then branch out from there. You want to spend your college years developing yourself as an expert and making yourself as marketable as possible to future employers or professional schools.
- Choose your major based on what you love to do and what you want to spend the next stage of your life doing, which will not necessarily bring home the fattest paycheck. Supplement your core requirements with classes you will enjoy or skills you would really like to have.
- Write outside of class in an effort to reflect and discover aspects about yourself that you may not have realized.
- Improve your writing every day.

FIVE

Study Like Your Grades Depend on It

Pop quiz. If it takes your Ma and Pa eighteen years to invest in your college education, how long can it take for you to flub it all up? Quick. I need an answer. *Eh!* Time's up. Answer? A few nights.

Not a year.

Not a semester.

Not even a week.

A few lazy nights.

By now you've come to appreciate that you're at an entirely new level academically. I'm glad we agree. But do you understand why? It's not because the material in college is more challenging or the professors are stricter with their grading techniques or everybody else just seems so much smarter than you, although all those are probably true. Quite simply, college is overwhelming. The material in college is indeed more challenging, and it just keeps coming. Professors are strict, and they don't care how hard you tried or how late you stayed up working. And for some reason, everybody else seems to "get it," while you're scrambling around campus trying to find a tutor. All that, and you still have to balance this crazy academic workload with all the other things you aim to accomplish and all that built-up ambition you have.

The worst of it is that, in certain situations, you might find yourself falling behind (a mere three days!) to the point that you might never catch up. Once you let a couple reading assignments fly by without notice or you get a poor grade on a heavily weighted exam, you could find yourself in deep enough that it won't even matter if the work you turn in for the rest of the semester is excellent.

This chapter aims to keep that from happening. After all, I'm not trying to scare you (although college really is going to kick your butt), but if you adopt the proper study techniques, you'll be hanging As on your minifridge and you'll need a separate calendar just so you can keep track of all your extra time.

Preparation

A Brave New World

You cruised through high school, no problem. As and Bs were a breeze, despite the fact you put in an absolute minimum amount of work for three years and virtually zero work during your senior year. Or maybe you actually exerted yourself through a rigorous academic schedule and are even bringing course credit with you to campus from all of those fancy-schmancy AP classes. Way to go, Champ.

But it doesn't matter. As I discussed in chapter 1, you aren't in high school anymore, so you have to prove yourself all over again. That goes for your social life, as well as your academic life. Your whole life. No one cares that you were the class geek in high school, always raising your hand with an eloquent answer or getting automatic bonus points just because your name is Steven Singh. (Steven Singh always got As just on reputation, that mother. But I'm not bitter.) You're the new kid, a statistic, and you've just been elected mayor of Nobodyville. Now, you've got to (or *get* to, depending on how you look at it) prove your geeky prowess all over again. You have to put in work. And vice versa if you were the class buffoon; here's your chance to make up for squandered years in the classroom.

Get Excited About Your Education

The trick—nay, the golden rule—is to get in the mind-set of being a scholar. You are a scholar now. Hell, you're in college. Everybody's a scholar. That's why you're here. But don't simply chase the best grades on campus, as if someone were keeping score; instead, own the material. I mean really get into it. Your mind-set should *not* be that you want to study for this economics exam because you could get an A; rather, you want to study for this economics exam because this is material that you want to know, and will need, for the rest of your life. Look—if you're putting in the work, you'll make the grade. But you want more. You should want to actually use this material in your life some day (even if they are requisite courses that you'll never use in "real life"). Too many people graduate with high GPAs but don't know what the hell they're talking about. Really. "I graduated with a 3.8 GPA, babe!" Sweet, where are you going to work? "Oh . . . well . . . uh . . . see . . . my . . . uh . . . interviews haven't . . . uh . . . really been going so well."

> I guess the paradox here is that you can get by with a solid GPA in college without learning much at all if you want to. Or, you can get excited about the material. Love it. Learn it because you want to learn it, not just because you want to impress your parents or an employer with an impressive transcript. That'll come with passion for the work you are doing.

Meet With Your Academic Advisor

You've already made best friends with your financial-aid advisor, and they're doing great things for you. Now it's time to make more friends. Yay, friends!

The next person you need to see—and get to know very well and meet with often—is your academic advisor. Their job is to help you register for (or drop or add) courses, help you declare a major, and make sure you are on track to graduate on time. That's about it. But if you take it one step further, this is another relationship whose well-being could correlate with your success and happiness as a college student. And that relationship really depends on you. Your advisor isn't going to chase you around campus, hoping to check in on how you're doing and how you're digging the college experience. "Havin' a good time, Jerome? How's that communications class I recommended?" No, sir. They have a flock of people to look after, and it isn't their job to babysit you. Which is fine and fair. But that doesn't mean you can't take this opportunity to really use your academic advisor as a valuable resource. They have inside information! And it's perfectly legal—and they want to give it to you. Come to your first meeting with a list of questions, comments, and concerns about the next four years. Probe them on the best and most beneficial courses to take within your potential major, the number of credits required for you to graduate, and what electives would make most sense for you. Ask for their recommendations for spreading your course load over four years. Ask them where to get answers that they don't have. And make sure you have their e-mail address cocked and ready to fire throughout the semester should an issue or question arise. They are there for you and can be a great support system if you choose to foster this relationship.

(Sidenote: Your advisor will be particularly useful when you *need* them. If you've built a healthy relationship, they'll be more apt to work with you when you start falling behind in a couple of courses, for example. You don't want them to strain to remember who you are when you come begging for assistance. You want them to say, "Hey, Vicki! What's happenin'? Come on in and have a seat. So, you're failing college algebra, eh? Let's see what we can do to help you out here."

[Sidenote to the sidenote: Your advisor is a resource. They are not the final answer. Mistakes happen, and it is very plausible that you could get to your senior year and discover that you missed that one required course because "my frickin' advisor didn't tell me to take it!" Calm down. It's not their responsibility. It's yours. Be your own advisor. Remember they have a hundred—or however many—other people they're looking after, so be sure to take control of your own future rather than leaving it to your advisor. Know the course catalogue and make a checklist of what you need to graduate.

{Sidenote to the third power: If you can tell that your advisor really isn't worth a damn, get a new one. It's a rare occurrence, but it could happen. So go to the dean and request a new advisor. Your school wants you to be successful, so they'll be happy to find someone who is a better fit for you.}])

Buying Books and Other School Supplies

I'm not quite sure I understand why college textbooks are so expensive. And I really don't understand why the authors of those textbooks receive pennies on the dollar from the sale of works that they wrote. Somebody's cashing in, but I'm not quite sure who. I'll do some research and get to the bottom of that. Meantime, though, it really doesn't matter why college textbook prices are so high. They are, and that's that. Just be prepared to factor that into your costs.

The surefire method of saving money on textbooks is to buy them used. As long as the pages aren't overly ravaged by so many markings you can't understand and digest the information (which very rarely happens) buying your textbooks secondhand can provide great value. A little highlighting here and there won't hurt, and it's the same information as a new version, with a much smaller price tag. (Just make sure you purchase the same edition as the one your professor wants you to use. The seventh edition your friend is trying to sell you might not suffice if it's the eighth edition that your professor is requesting.) And definitely look online for books before you visit your college bookstore. College bookstores will murder your bank account, but you can get a discount from Half.com or on Amazon, especially if you're buying used. Heck, you might even be able to make a little money in the deal when it comes time to resell those books. Be aware of the shipping costs on Internet orders, though. A twelve-dollar book might look like a steal, but when it turns into nineteen dollars after shipping, you might have been better off elsewhere. Note also, when you're ordering online, make sure to get a list of books before class starts so you can allow time for the books to arrive via snail mail. You don't want to spend two weeks without a book just because they're slow to work their way through the postal system.

Sharing textbooks with people you meet in your classes can also save you a ton of money, but be careful that you don't find yourself wasting valuable study time by trotting all over campus in the snow just to pick up a book for a couple hours. It won't be worth it. Buddy up with people in your residence hall, and you'll save time and money (and probably even have a study partner).

Of course there are all kinds of other school supplies you need to have at your disposal. Well, kind of. The number and variety of school supplies you purchase is totally up to you. You can get by with a couple pens and a few notepads (I did), but it might not be the best idea for your organization or production. You might want to get different colored pens and a Five Star notebook for every class and rulers and a calculator and a stapler and a Trapper Keeper and a green backpack with a secret compartment to store your personal digital assistant, and . . . and . . . and . . . which is cool. But buy supplies that fit into your system of time management and studying. If you want to take notes on a legal pad and then transfer those notes to your computer later, then do it. It doesn't matter that your friend Noah is taking notes directly on his computer. Have your own system, and buy the supplies you need to fit that system.

Cheating as a Lost Art

Sadly, cheating happens. A lot. And it has become even easier over the years with the development of all types of new technology. With all these new gadgets and wireless contraptions, it's not only easy to cheat, but it's difficult for professors to catch you (and prove that you cheated). It won't take much brainstorming on your part to figure out how to cheat.

If you're unclear about the definition of cheating in college, it's pretty simple: any unfair advantage that you have that your peers do not (and that your professor would not approve of) is cheating. So, that extends beyond just writing out a cheat sheet or stealing test files or buying a research paper. You should double-check with your professor and the university regulations if you're not sure. One professor might allow you to review the old exam from when your friend took the class, but another may view that as cheating.

If you get caught cheating, you're toast. They'll send you home, no second chances. But that's not the angle I'm taking here. If you're worried about getting caught, then you're not worried about the right things. (And if you're worried about it in the first place, it's probably cheating.) Look—if you're cheating now, at this stage of your life, what kind of precedent are you setting for your future? This isn't eighth grade anymore, and you aren't peeking at your neighbor's test "to make sure they chose the right answer, too." This is the big time. You're a grown person and you need to make grown-person decisions. If you cheat now on a homework assignment, you'll cheat next month on an exam. If you start cheating on schoolwork now, you're defining yourself as dishonest and you'll end up cheating at your job and cheating on your wife and . . . . Hey, I'm not kidding. This is serious business here. You're defining your future *right now.*

Besides, in the end, you're just cheating yourself anyway. (Ha! Cheating yourself. I wonder if any of these crappy puns are getting past my editor.) But really, you are cheating yourself. If you are cheating to get by in college, then you clearly don't have the desire to learn. And if you don't have the desire to learn, then what are you doing here in the first place? Really. You should be soaking this information up and cramming it into your head because you—or somebody—is paying lots and lots of money for this information. Learning is fun and knowledge is fun! You're building the foundation for the rest of your life—*right now.* And you're not gaining anything by cheating. Cheating? Are you serious? Do you think people who cheat succeed? (Fair enough, the answer to that question is definitely yes. There are plenty of successful dishonest people out there. Some get caught, and some don't. I, personally, just can't imagine living a life where I have to look over my shoulder every day, and I certainly can't imagine a life where I look at my accomplishments and think, "I didn't really earn that. I cheated.") Cheating now sets you up for failure in the future.

Enough said. That was your lecture for this chapter. I hope you were paying attention!

Don't Procrastinate

Make the decision—here and now—that you will not procrastinate. It's that simple. *Make the decision.* It's like quitting smoking cold turkey. It isn't easy, but just do it. Pride yourself on getting your work done now rather than saving it for later. It will save you all kinds of headaches, and it will most certainly have a positive impact on your grades. (The last time I procrastinated in college was also the last time I earned a C. I saved all my studying for Philosophy until the end of the semester, and it cost me. Lesson learned.)

The trick to avoiding procrastination is to get the big projects out of the way first. This goes for everything, from getting your assignments completed to studying to taking some tougher classes your freshman year. Start big; finish small. Start hard; finish easy. If you do the reverse, you'll find yourself getting so mentally frazzled that you'll really start to procrastinate. "*Ugh,* I still have all of that work to do? I'll just start it later tonight or tomorrow. Or after the weekend."

It's important to start larger projects as soon as they are assigned. Get something (anything) done the very first day. At the very least, take twenty minutes to get organized. This will allow you to get your work done better and faster. Just as with studying—as we've discussed briefly and will examine deeper shortly—you are more effective when you work in spurts rather than saving it all for one cram session. So, if you have a twenty-page research paper due in four weeks, budget five pages a week, for example. If you delay, you'll be tossing together worthless writing that will leave you frustrated that you waited until the last minute.

If you happen to procrastinate by nature, that just means that you have poor time-management techniques. No worries. Go back and review chapter 2 and develop an organizational plan that works for you. Set easier, more reachable short-term goals, and work from there. Develop a routine and manage your progress. Eat right and sleep right. All these are techniques that can help you avoid procrastination. And once you get started, you'll be able to ride the momentum from one project to the next.

Besides, just like smoking or any other bad habit, once you've kicked procrastination for a couple weeks, you'll never go back to that lifestyle.

Schedule Your Tougher Courses Now

Working with your academic advisor, you can set up your course load in such a way that you maximize your potential in the classroom without getting burned out. College courses are challenging—very challenging—but the absolute worst thing you can do is run away from them by dillydallying during your freshman year or piling up introductory-level courses just so you can "get adjusted." Intro courses are fine (especially if they satisfy core requirements), but they also don't represent the more challenging courses that you will have to take later on. My recommendation is to dive in headfirst from day one. Work on your prerequisites, sure, but don't dodge or delay the more advanced courses on your "to take" list. You will not only be happy that you forced yourself to develop a college mind-set, but you'll thank me during your senior year, when you are cruising through a lighter course load and your friends are complaining that they may never graduate.

Class Time

Classroom time is the most important time of your college career. Well, in fairness, I shouldn't single out any one time as "the most important time of your college career." You need to study; you need to network; you need to go out on the town with your friends . . . you need balance. But class time can end up being the most valuable part of your academic achievement. You can make up for lost study time or lost social time or most of your other lost time, but you can't make up for lost class time. So get your butt out of bed and trudge your way on over to that early morning class that you were forced to sign up for because it was the last one available.

The First Day of Class

I love the first day of class. It's my favorite day. New classes, new people, new material to learn, and new opportunities. Last semester I did terribly, and this semester I get the chance to make up for it. The first day of class is my opportunity to set the precedent for the coming semester. My confidence is soaring on the first day of class. I'm untouchable. And you will be, too.

The one strategy that I used during my upperclassmen years (that I wish I had used during my first two years) was to sit in the front row of the class, every class. I know your parents told you and your high school coach told you and the guy who came to speak to you at orientation told you. And now I'm telling you: *sit in front.* It not only lets the professor know that you mean business, but it also allows you to center your attention on the task at hand rather than focusing on the fidgeting going on in the rest of the classroom. Sitting in front equals greater performance. No joke.

Also, on the first day of class, take time to digest what kind of commitment this course is going to require. If it doesn't seem like the right fit for you, drop it now rather than withdrawing—and taking a hit on your transcript—later. As soon as your first class of each subject is over (or at least at some point that same day), transfer the dates from your syllabus to your planner, organizer, or calendar. This will allow you to analyze the bigger picture of what you can expect from that class throughout the semester.

Oh yeah! And don't forget to introduce yourself to your professor . . .

Know Your Professors

This is a strategy I picked up playing basketball in college. Most of us dismissed the "scholar" portion of "scholar-athlete," so we had to do everything possible to cut whatever (legal) corners would give us an advantage in the classroom. And the first thing that Coach would say (well, second after, "Shep, when is your sorry ass going to start playing defense?") was how important it was for us to introduce ourselves to each of our professors. Shake their hand, tell them who you are, and ask them when a good time would be to approach them with any issues that might arise throughout the semester. Which might happen or might not. You may breeze through the course without issue, or you may struggle and end up meeting with them on a weekly basis. In either event, it's valuable to take the opportunity to meet them ahead of time. *You want them to know who you are.* When they are grading your tests or your essays, you want them to have a mental picture of you. And if you stop by their office once in a while, you never know when they might tell you to "make sure you know the major points in chapter 8 for the exam next Tuesday." Be frank and ask them what it will take to get a solid grade in their class. This is the advantage you are giving yourself by sitting in the front of the class and by getting to know your professors. If you don't, you can forget getting any kind of assistance late in the semester when you don't understand a certain concept or you need just one more day for an assignment. "Who are you again, and which class of mine are you taking?" Your credibility can, in fact, be worth a letter grade. I've seen it happen, and so have your professors.

Academically, your professors are your greatest allies. They've been where you are and they know what you're going through. They can help you with all kinds of decisions, from choosing your course of study to the best way to structure a research paper. As long as you show that you are genuinely interested in learning, professors are happy to help.

These relationships can also extend beyond academic assistance. I would sit with professors for coffee or lunch just to discuss current events. A lot of them came to my basketball games at Merrimack. I studied in Spain on a trip that my Spanish professor set up. When I published *Scratch Beginnings,* I got all kinds of support from the professors whom I had befriended in college. A lot of them came to hear me speak on campuses, and I know I sold at least five books from the relationships I maintained since graduation (and still maintain today). *Cha-ching!*

Let me be clear: you are not trying to be a suck-up. You're not lobbying for a B+ instead of a B. Don't leave an apple on their desk or wink at them when you say, "Nice to meet you." Sitting in front of the class works to your benefit; introducing yourself to your professor allows you to become more acquainted. That's it. Nothing else. You want to know that you can count on them if necessary and, alternately, let them know that they can count on you if they need anything. Don't read too much into it, but don't devalue it, either.

Don't Skip Class (Ever!)

So, there you are on the first day of class, and you're so excited you've got butterflies. And then comes the second class. And the third. By the fourth class, the luster tends to wear off (although not always), and you're just not as excited as you were on day one. The assignments have started to roll in, your professor isn't as nice as he seemed at first, and that cute guy in the second row has transferred out. Welcome to life, kid. You get used to something, you get bored, and you want to move on. But that doesn't mean you can. You can't just give up or start shedding effort just because you're not enjoying yourself or your life is losing flavor. That goes for a lot of things—your marriage, your job, a stick of Juicy Fruit gum—and going to class is one of them.

Even if there's not a required attendance policy, go to class. Heck, forget the attendance policy altogether. You're not going to class to get points; that's a bonus. You're in class because you're pumped to be filling your head with all of this juicy knowledge. Bring it on! More than that, your class participation (whether it's graded or not) depends on you sitting there, front and center, with your hand raised. Again, this isn't kissing up. You raise your hand because you are curious why each chromosome in the human body carries a different genetic load. Nothing more. There should be no ulterior motive for you going to class every day, other than the fact that you know how valuable this information is for your grade and for your future. Most private-school classes cost over a dollar a minute (according to the unofficial math experiment I just did on my computer's calculator), and public institutions aren't much cheaper these days. So make the most of it! (Even when you're sick or you don't feel like going.)

"But Adam, I can just get the notes from my friend Dingleberry, who's in the class with me. And furthermore, all the slides from class are posted online. See, I don't even need to go!" *Eh!* Wrong. You never know what's going to happen in class. Something pertinent to your grade is going to happen in every class—whether it's an engaging discussion or a series of notes you won't get from Dingleberry or a change of test dates—and you don't want to miss it. Perhaps you can make up a lot in college, but *you can't make up a missed class.* Class attendance equals preparation.

If you absolutely have to miss a class because you are playing in the NBA All-Star Celebrity Game or you got shot in a drive-by, e-mail your professor ahead of time. They will be very confused. "Uh . . . uh . . . okay, just . . . uh . . . make sure to . . . uh . . . do the reading." Students *never* e-mail to say they're going to miss a class, but here you are again, setting yourself apart from the crowd. (*Yes.* The answer to your question—"Do I really want to set myself apart from the crowd?"—is *yes.*)

Going to *every* class is real-world preparation. Your day is going to start before 8 a.m. once you graduate, and you can't just sleep through work because you stayed up too late the night before.

Most important, if you go to class, it will be very difficult for you to fail. I can't make any guarantees, but—well, wait . . . yes, I can: if you go to class, you will not fail. I guarantee it. There you go. I said it. It's as if you'll be working your way up from a C instead of an F. Really. This is the power of going to class (and paying attention!). Test questions come from lectures, and lectures happen *in class.* Go to class.

And while you're there, why not take a note or two . . .

Take Notes (Every Day)

Going to class is one thing, but making the most of your class time is another. It's great to sit there and really digest all the information that your professor spits at you, but do you really think you'll remember *everything* tomorrow? Hell, you'll forget most of it when you leave for a bathroom break. So, the key then, to ensure that you will be able to review the information later, is simple: Write it down. Take notes. And take good notes. Now, I could sit here and give you plenty of tips on note-taking, but it would be futile. Everybody has their own system of jotting down ideas. Maybe you use bullet points. Or maybe you write in paragraph form. Or maybe you have some secret shorthand language that only you can decipher. Super. Just as long as you are writing down the main points and ideas of your professor's lecture, that's all that matters.

Then, when it comes time to study your notes, it will be like skipping immediately to the review session. You already know this stuff! You can really cut down on your study time a lot by going to class and taking notes. Rather than reading every chapter word for word, you might be able to just skim through (like you're probably doing with this book right now) with a highlighter to pick up a few detailed points—since you already have a pretty good idea of the subject matter.

Study Time

Gone (for the most part) are the days of multiple-choice tests, but of course you are already mentally prepared for the academic challenges and demands that the next four years will present. Every one of us who attends college puts in an ungodly number of hours with our noses in the books and typing away at the computer, but the difference comes with those who know how to study right. There are essentially two kinds of people who go to college: those who study hard and those who study smart. *The best grades don't go to the smartest, just to those who study the smartest.* Anybody can just start reading and taking notes, but not everybody can do this effectively. So, before you even crack open that first textbook and nestle in for a long night of studying, take a moment or two to develop effective study habits.

Develop Your Study System

My college roommate Bruno spent tons of time studying. He would read a chapter and highlight key points, take notes, make flash cards, and then review it all with a group of his classmates the evening before a major test. Me? I just read and highlighted. My other roommate, Lightfoot, just took notes. Of course, it helped that Light and I had easier majors, while Bruno was working his way through the grueling sports-medicine program, but the point is that we each developed our own (usually creative!) system that worked for each of us.

Just as I discussed with your time-management and organizational techniques, it is important to develop your own system for studying. You might learn by writing out important information, while others prefer to visualize when they read. Flash cards and mnemonics might work for some people but not for others. Maybe you create a quiz-show format to test yourself on all the notes you have taken for a particular exam. Or maybe you have some cognitive gift where you can just read the information, digest and store it all, and forgo note-taking altogether.

In any event, while it's important to enter college with a good idea of what kind of study system will work for you (perhaps using a similar system to what you used in high school—as long as it was successful), keep in mind that your system might not be as effective as you originally thought. Your first test could overwhelm you and force you to rethink your system altogether. Fine. No problem. A developing and improving study system is better than diving in with no system at all. If you move forward without one, you'll lose yourself worrying how long it could take you to finish studying and if you are even studying right in the first place. Organize your study time and you're saving time, energy, and in the end, your grades.

Start Studying Well Beforehand

There are a couple techniques that are imperative to whatever study system you've formulated for yourself, no matter how you choose to tackle the books. One is making the decision that you will start studying well in advance of an expected test date. *The worst thing you can do is to start studying the day before.* The worst! The same rules that applied to starting big projects early, as I mentioned before, stand true here. Quite simply, it is more effective to learn material in small bits over time rather than trying to cram loads of information into your head the night before. (I'm not talking out of my backside here. These are scientific facts that have been researched by scientists who study the science of studying.) Starting to study in advance will save you time and headaches, and it will definitely show when grades come out.

Now, even if you spend a week or two or three consistently preparing for a test, an extended review session will be in order the night before an exam. Of course. But this is not cramming. Use your best judgment to determine how much work you need to put into studying for a particular class. Intro to History might be a cinch for you, so you have to study only an hour a day for a week and review for two hours the night before test day. Philosophy 201, on the other hand, is killing you, so you might need to put in an hour a day for two weeks and three hours the night (or two) before. Spreading out your studying doesn't mean you won't have to get serious the night before an exam, but it does make those few days before the exam a whole hell of a lot easier—not to mention more effective.

Physical Preparation

So, here you are on test day. You've put in all kinds of hours studying. You've read, you've highlighted, and you've reviewed notes in between sets at the gym. You are a professor's dream. Very nice. Now comes the tough part: physically preparing yourself to endure that exam that you are already absolutely 100 percent mentally prepared to take.

Think about how your body and mind perform when you are at your physical peak. You're a machine; nothing can stop you. You've spent all this time preparing for the main event, and now, here it is. Don't screw up all that mental preparation just because you failed to prepare yourself physically. Get a good night's sleep; eat a nutritious breakfast and lunch; work out; relax; free your body, and free your mind. There's no sense in trying to squeeze the material into your head at this point. You've either taken the time to learn it or you haven't. Now, relax. A well-rested and well-fed (and therefore, confident) body and mind will produce better answers in a quicker amount of time. A lethargic mind will struggle to get anything on paper at all, and even then, those strained answers will be a load of garbage. If you've studied smart leading up to the exam, your physical preparation before the exam will be a cakewalk.

A Few Words on Group Study

The social aspect of college is, of course, the most fun. Whether you're sitting around doing nothing with your friends or scurrying about the campus from party to party, your leisure life represents the amusement, while your academic life represents the mundane. So, here's an idea: why not combine the two? Ah, brilliant!

Be careful, though. Just as everyone has their own unique study system, there can be pros and cons to studying in a group. Pros? You don't have to hold yourself accountable for as much material, since you'll be reviewing all the information when your study group meets. Five minds tend to be stronger than one, and if you have any questions or you're stuck on a topic, somebody in the group can possibly help you figure it out. And, indeed, studying in groups is much less tedious than sitting by yourself in your lonely room, sifting through pages and pages of notes. Cons? Social time is great, but not much gets accomplished when you end up sitting around chatting about who's dating whom. You could end up being well versed on certain topics but knowing only a little about others (and you never know which topics are more important for the exam in the first place). Getting started could be a problem, as well: "Hey, you guys wanna grab a cup of coffee and download a few songs before we get started?" Moreover, getting the right people together is a challenge in itself. So:

> Make your own decision whether you're going to study in a group. Try it once or twice, just to see how it works for you. If it strikes you as a productive exercise, keep doing it. If you can't measure how it's helping you, revert back to studying solo. Me? I always made sure to find a balance between

group study and individual study, with heavier weight on
the latter. I would find a private secluded area where I could
study by myself without any distractions, and then I would
use a group-study session as a way to review what I'd spent
time studying individually. Experiment to see what works for
you.

Hot Study Tips

So that gives you a general idea of what you can be doing to
prepare for your next exam. But those are methods that *everybody* is using. You want to set yourself apart. You want to go
above and beyond and study like no one else is studying. You
want (need!) to study smart.

There are three techniques, which I learned (late) moving
through college, that became my golden rules for exam preparation. (If you haven't figured this out yet, exams are your
grades in college. Papers and essays count, too, depending on
the class, but you can't depend on quiz grades to buoy your
average, and you definitely aren't going to get credit for doing
ordinary homework assignments like you did in high school.
Exams—often just two or three throughout the semester—are
heavily weighted to compose your final grade.) Indeed, if I had
understood and employed these three techniques sooner, academic success would have come much easier for me.

Shadow the Geeks

In high school, there was little glory in being the smartest kid
in the class. That was the person who always got picked on and
sneered at in the hallway, especially if they did everything they

could to make it known that they were the most intelligent. It was lonely at the top. Right now, though, that kid (if it isn't you in the first place) is your best friend. Find them and join forces.

It might take you a little while—they won't be wearing a sign that says, ASK ME! I PROBABLY KNOW THE ANSWER!— but you can find them. Ask around who got the best grade. If you've been fostering a healthy relationship with your professor, ask who got the best grade on the last test. Maybe they'll tell you; maybe they won't. But it's worth asking. At the very least, they will likely let you know which students to shadow. Or pay attention in class to see who always seems to know the answers. *The professors want you to find that person because they want you to do well.*

This is the person (or people if you can pinpoint a group of geniuses) whom you want on your team. Get in their study group. Find out how they study. Exchange notes. Ask them questions. (They probably know the right answers.) Take them out for drinks. Send flowers just because it's Tuesday. I'm telling you: you are who you hang with. *Hang with smarties and become a smartie.*

Between knowing my professors and meeting the smart people in the class, college became so much easier for me. I can remember exam days when everybody else would be walking to class with notes in their hand, trying to jam information into their brains at the last moment, and I would just peer across the room at the smart kids and smile, as if we were in on some brilliant scheme. But it wasn't a scheme. They knew the material, and so did I, because I had put myself in that position.

Thirty- to Forty-Five-Minute Block Studying

Studying really isn't that bad. Actually, it's kind of fun if you carry the attitude that time spent buried in the books is time spent becoming more intelligent and discovering new information that you can use forever. Love to learn. Now, is studying tough? Yeah. Grueling? Sometimes. Monotonous? Well, it doesn't have to be.

Break your study time into chunks. I've mentioned thirty to forty-five minutes because that's what works for me. I just can't sit still any longer than that. Thirty minutes actually might be kind of short; maybe it's not enough time to absorb a chunk of material. Forty-five minutes to an hour may work better for you, but in any event, go until you catch your mind drifting, and then take a five- to ten-minute break. Grab a snack, run a lap around the building, do a couple hundred push-ups . . . whatever. Just do something to break that monotony. Give yourself time to digest the information without being overwhelmed, and then jump right back in where you left off. You'll return with a fresh, energized mind, rather than dragging on for hours on end. Five one-hour sessions are far more effective than two two-and-a-half-hour sessions, or worse, one long five-hour session.

Don't take long breaks. Going to dinner or working out at the gym or watching a movie will undermine the idea behind studying in small chunks. You don't want to lose your train of thought. If you're studying between classes, for example, make sure you are just reviewing or that you bring closure to the material before you move on. Reading and highlighting a chapter all the way through can be effective, but stopping halfway—and trying to pick back up later—might be counterproductive.

Reading Right

It is going to be quite an eye-opening experience when you receive your syllabi on the first day of classes and you see all the reading you have to do. It is incredible. I, for one, remember thinking that there was no possible way I could complete all those reading assignments on time. If your question is, How the heck am I going to read all these books that I bought for my classes?, you're not going to get your answer from your professors. They don't care that you are now being forced to do more reading in a shorter amount of time than you ever thought possible. Somehow, though, the reading you don't do will end up on the exam. Murphy's Law. Welcome to the real world.

You *can* do *all* this reading in a short amount of time and still spend time developing a life beyond books. It's what college is about: balance. And there are no shortcuts on either the social or the academic side; both require work.

Productive reading involves three steps:

1. Read the material thoroughly. Go through it and just take it all in. Read the headings and the chapter review *before* you get started so you'll have an idea of the important terms to look for.
2. Skim back through and highlight key points. Take notes in the margins. Ask yourself: What appear to be the key points? What do you think my professor wants me to carry forward from this chapter to the test? And then answer yourself.
3. Move your highlighted material to notes or note cards or both, whatever works for you. By now, you're beginning to get a solid grasp on the material, but this will give you

the opportunity to quiz yourself or review it on a whim, whenever you would like. And simply by writing out the pertinent information, you'll be giving your brain another chance to absorb it.

Whatever you do, make sure you do the reading before class time. You don't want to be that person sitting around with a dazed look on your face since you don't know what the heck is going on. It will be frustrating for you, your professor, and your classmates. At the very least, have an idea of the key terms and phrases before you go into the lecture: "The antiferromagnetic phase of spins on atomic lattices!" "Well, no, not even close, but thank you for doing the reading." In any event, it will make note-taking during class much easier, and it will bring better results to your future reading assignments.

If You Fall Behind, Get Help

If, after you have exhausted all sorts of energy developing your own system, you still aren't doing well in your classes—get help. It's that simple. If you don't suck up your pride here, you're going to continue to fall further behind, perhaps to a point where you won't be able to recover. There are all kinds of academic resources available to you on campus, and you're already paying top dollar for them. So use them! Consult your academic advisor (who is, by now, a close friend of yours) or the tutoring center or the academic-achievement center or whatever other resource you can track down, and ask where you can get a helping hand before you fall off the map.

Chapter in Brief

Okey dokey, let's review:

- Prepare for your academic life by building a solid foundation. Buy books (lightly used) and really get to know your academic advisor. Schedule your tougher courses now.
- Get serious about not cheating and not procrastinating. This is your education!
- It all starts the first day of class: take hardcore notes and meet your professors.
- Develop your own best study system. Experiment with group study to determine if it is effective for you.
- Prepare yourself physically for studying and for taking tests. Eat right; sleep right; live right.
- Surround yourself with the smart kids, and you'll become a smart kid, too.
- Study in short bursts rather than one long marathon session. Become an effective reader.

SIX

Taking Initiative, Getting Involved

College is tough enough academically without having to worry about putting work into the other aspects of your life. But now (now!) is the ideal time to refine and upgrade those. "Geez, Shep. I just spent almost two days straight digging through trig and economics and English comp assignments and now I have to get out there and get involved in something? Why? What's the point?"

Some of you may be going to college for just an education. You intend to graduate with a 4.0 and go on to a prestigious graduate school before entering a profession that's going to kick out a fat paycheck. Super. But let's back up here a minute. Do you really want to be that mechanical with these crucial years of your life, looking back years later at your college experience and wondering, "What if?" Do you really want to go through these next four years without getting involved in student government or a fraternity or sorority or a service organization? Don't you want to know what it's like to compete on the intramural courts and fields? And are you really going to graduate without taking a summer or semester or year to study outside of the United States? Really?

Here's your chance to become a part of something bigger than yourself, take initiative, and get involved. You have the opportunity over these next four years to join a group or organization (or even start one on your own) and to make a difference in the lives of your college community and beyond. You may be a big fish in a small pond or bait in a lake, but either way, here's your chance to leave your mark. Here's where *The Best Four Years* comes into play. Don't let your diploma be your lone accomplishment by graduation time. *Do something more.*

Join a Club or Organization

The simplest advice I can give you here is to just get after it. Dig in, and don't look back. Just do it. It's going to be tough to make any mistakes here because you are going to end up doing what you want to do rather than what you have to do. This is the fun part! So treat it as such. By joining a club or organization that interests you, you're going to meet "your kind of people," you're going to make a difference, and you're going to look back at your college years with a smile. "Those were the days."

Too many times I talk to parents whose children never joined a club or organization. And the same was true as I looked around at my peers at Merrimack. I don't get it. There was a distinct separation between those who joined something and those who didn't. Some kids would come back after class and play video games all afternoon and others were *making things happen* in their little niches on campus. There were the joiners, and then there was everybody else. I'm sure you can imagine my frustration as an RA. It was like pulling teeth trying to get my floor to attend programs. Some kids—the same kids—attended every activity, while I could count on others to never come. Guess who graduated with more impressive GPAs and résumés, and guess who graduated without notice? You want to be different here, folks, to stand out. You want people—professors, peers, administrators, cheerleaders . . . everybody—talking about you behind your back. "Hey, did you hear what Francisco did? That guy started his own chapter of Habitat for Humanity right here on campus. Pretty impressive." Get ambitious and follow through with that ambition.

> More than anything, getting involved in a club or organization (during your first week on campus!) is going to complement your academic life nicely. If you are struggling to fill your idle time (with idle activities), you'll become apathetic, but if you stay busy and engaged in the community, confidence will be contagious, from one area of your life to the next.

Go to the Activities Fair

There are plenty of ways to find out what's going on around campus and what your campus has to offer for involvement. Fliers abound, your e-mail inbox is full, and the college newspaper is screaming with all kinds of opportunity to get involved on campus. My recommendation, though, is to head over to the campus activities fair and peruse what each organization has to offer. This is effective because not only is it one-stop shopping, but also because you can get firsthand answers on the spot. Here, you can discuss the prospects (activities, expectations, requirements, meeting times, et cetera) of each organization in which you are interested and begin to decide if that organization is for you. Your intuition is your strongest ally when deciding on an organization to join. And it's tough to make any kind of determination from a flier or an e-mail. After all, you're looking for a comfortable fit here, and if a club president strikes you as smug or otherwise aggravating, you might want to move on.

The activities fair, which usually occurs only at the start of each school year, is ideal for scoping out what's available to you. At the very least, you'll be meeting new people and picking up a few free goodies, since many organizations will entice you with snacks or key chains or Frisbees. Take an appetite and a bag with you and prepare to clean up.

Religious and Cultural Organizations

When I left for Merrimack (which, by the way, is a devoutly Catholic institution), I wasn't religious and I didn't care about one culture versus another. I just saw us all living in harmony; you've got your beliefs and I've got mine. Cool. Then, I began to see how important (and fascinating!) it was to learn about other people and the stories they had to tell. So, since I was already passionate about learning Spanish, and I have something of a penchant for Latin women, I joined the Latinos Club (as the token gringo).

Since I wasn't really affiliated with any religion or culture, joining the Latinos Club allowed me to broaden my knowledge a little, to become more cultured if you will. And to meet Latinas. Maybe, though, you do have strong religious convictions or are interested in connecting and socializing with people "just like you." There are organizations at your college for you to do just that. Jewish? Join Hillel, and you will be able to share experiences and holidays and participate in Jewish activities. African-American? Asian? Buddhist? Baptist? Join the club.

This can also be a great way for you to educate others on your religious or cultural roots. Invite people to your group's events and share your knowledge with them. Ask questions of your own and answer theirs. And when it comes time for you to attend someone else's event, go! I'm not asking you to convert to Judaism. Just walk in with an open mind and walk out informed and maybe even enlightened.

Joining a religious or cultural organization is a great way to maintain your faith or culture. There are plenty of negative forces fighting to lead you astray during college, but your peers can be there to support you, now that you are away from the familiar surroundings of your home life.

There is no question that I am a better educated and stronger person for joining the Latinos Club. I was able to practice my Spanish, maximize my (low) salsa dancing potential, and learn that various cultures have both fascinating differences and striking similarities. And meet Latin ladies. Align your interests, but feel free to inflate your comfort zone a little when considering which organization you would like to join.

Service Organizations

"Give and ye shall receive" is not a mantra that applies just to Christmas gift giving or late nights with your sweetheart. Your college years (and then again, the years when you're old and wrinkly and bored to tears from the monotony of retirement) provide the ideal platform for you to give back to a community that has already given you so much (obviously, or you wouldn't be in college in the first place). You're young and energetic, and you need a worthy outlet for all that youth and energy. Joining a service organization can be that worthy outlet.

Some of you may already have experience with community service from your days of volunteerism, or as punishment for shooting your neighbor in the face with a paintball gun when you were fourteen. (Hey, he started it. And, Robert Cochran, if you're reading this, know that if I ever see you on my front lawn again, I will start firing without warning.) So whether it was required by law or you and your friends and family wanted to lend a hand, you probably have an idea how rewarding community service involvement can be.

This is one area where there most certainly will not be any shortage of organizations. And if your favorite or ideal organization isn't on campus, you can find them close by. You can volunteer at a shelter or a library or with a group that picks up trash on the highway. You can waltz on over to a local elementary or middle school and give an hour or two per week to assist students with their assignments. Those of you who are more ambitious can join an organization like Big Brothers Big Sisters, where your mentoring skills can really be utilized, or Habitat for Humanity, where you can devote time to building houses (either locally or in exotic locations throughout the world). Many colleges around the country have Alternative Spring Break options, where you can spend your week helping someone less fortunate than yourself—abroad or domestically—instead of going to the beach to vote on wet T-shirt contests. At the end of the week, you bring home the priceless feeling of pride rather than the pricey (and itchy) feeling of a sexually transmitted infection (STI).

If you're totally lost on where you can get involved, most

campuses have a volunteer office—or you can latch on with a professor to do community work that aligns with your major. Many professors will even offer extra credit for volunteer service, which can be a huge academic bonus.

As an athlete and an RA, I put in a ton of volunteer hours, especially during the last two years of my college tenure, but I really wish I had gotten involved sooner. Once you start to meet such wonderful people and see the impact you're able to make, it can become the most fun and rewarding time of your college life.

Greek Life

On most campuses, the most established organizations are fraternities and sororities. The extent to which they are represented on campus varies—at some schools, Greek life can rule the social arena, where on other campuses they don't have as profound a standing—but no matter where you go to school (unless you're getting your degree online), Greek organizations will likely exist to some degree. It's tough to know what to expect from each individual fraternity or sorority, so it is important to ask around and learn about your options (outside the fraternity or sorority itself). Some Greek institutions live up to the reputation of hazing and partying and no work, but you'll find that most have a stringent set of principles and respect their responsibilities to the college community. Know what you're getting into before you pledge.

Going Greek can make the transition into college much easier, since you'll have instant companionship in your new group of brothers or sisters. Upperclassmen can serve as mentors—it will be tough to find more allegiant academic support anywhere else on campus—and the alumni of your fraternity or sorority can serve as your first great network. "Ah! You're from the DKE house? My goodness. Come on in! Of course I can set up an interview for you." And getting involved around campus often becomes easier for those that have pledged: many Greek members hold high office in clubs or organizations throughout campus, and community service is often a requirement for your membership. There's no question that on many campuses, Greek membership commands respect.

On the other hand, don't neglect the demands of joining a fraternity or sorority. Often, Greek membership can be expensive and time-consuming. Monthly dues can add up quickly, and you'll still need money to buy food and drinks for parties or T-shirts for intramural football. Moreover, if you plan to actually live in your fraternity or sorority house, you're talking about a serious expense. And that's just the financial side. Greek life also requires a commitment to attend mandatory activities and events and meetings. These are not "go when you feel like it" type gatherings, either. It's all or nothing, so be prepared for a full-time undertaking if this is the route you decide to take.

My friend Mike Kelly, who had the big-school experience at Florida State University, has some fascinating stories to tell about his Greek adventures. Indeed, he has to hold some to himself, but here is Mike describing how much he appreciated being in a fraternity:

The decision to join a fraternity or sorority should not be taken lightly. Greek life does come with its own set of stigmas. The "independents" on campus can view joining as buying friends. Each fraternity and sorority also has its own stereotype. Don't think having letters makes you instantly cool; you must pick your house wisely. Your house can actually make you the butt of jokes in and out of the Greek system. It's not uncommon to hear people say things like, "If you can't go Greek, go TKE," or, "She must be DG because she goes down as fast as an anchor." The many-times unfair slogans vary from school to school, and no house is immune. You should pick the house that represents who you are and who you want to be. Be prepared; each house is looking for someone who will fit in. Know that, from the moment you walk up, the selection process is at work and has many layers. For example, in my house, the first layer came from our friendly female greeters. The greeters were girls from our favorite sororities. Always smiling, seemingly friendly to all, they had a secret role that only the brothers knew. As a potential pledge walked up, they would smile, ask them their name and where they were from, and give them a name badge. If the girls thought they were hot, they wrote their name in all caps; if they were not good-looking enough, then lowercase. That meant every brother who spoke to that potential pledge knew what the girls thought and could bias their opinion. No brother wanted the house to be thought of as average or unattractive. It is also important to note that just because the girls liked you at the door didn't mean you were in the clear. Many a "loser" had been known to sneak past the girls and fail miserably. That is why many houses won't extend bids the first night of pledge week. I remember one kid who, from first impression, looked like he was a lock. He was good-looking, personable, athletic: a great fit—until the after party. After a few drinks, his evil cocky twin came out! The once easygoing, put-together stud became a sloppy, groping, slurring chick stalker, not knowing how to handle himself and making everyone around him uncomfortable. He went from a being a yes to being kicked out of the party, yelling, "What? What did I do? What!"

"Going Greek" isn't as superficial and pretentious as it may sound. The selection process is an imperfect but necessary evil. The young men and women chosen are no longer just some guys or girls on campus. Rather, they represent a whole group. Their actions from then on could impact the whole house. I remember the feeling of receiving my bid. I was a freshman at a new school, not sure about myself or my future. Getting my bid reinforced a self-confidence that I needed and reassured me that I had a support system. I had others who saw the great things in me that I saw. Through the pledge process, I bonded with my fellow pledge brothers whom I could relate to. The brothers taught us that anything worth wanting required hard work, and we had to prove we deserved initiation. We were expected to be well-rounded gentlemen. For example, when a woman entered the house, everyone in the room was expected to stand in recognition. We had a responsibility to not only ourselves but to the brotherhood. "Bros before . . ." all others! I had a semester-long pledgeship that taught me lessons of humility, responsibility, compassion, loyalty, and commitment, to name a few. Those lessons often came in unorthodox ways, many of which can be shared only with fellow brothers. Some may have called our activities "hazing" and, to outside eyes, could be misunderstood. Some activities became the stuff of school myth and legend. All I can say about pledgeship is I never did anything that those before me didn't do, my morals were never compromised, and it was the most fun I never want to do again.

Once initiated, the fraternity was my on-campus family and an invaluable resource. The hundred-plus-man house was filled with men I loved and respected. Our house was ground zero for anything and everything you wanted to do. We were involved in community service, athletics, student government, and every major on campus. Our elected social chair posted and updated a calendar full of official fraternity functions, ensured we had the best seats at sporting events, and posted a list of the best parties on campus. We had a personal library full of notes, papers, and exams from classes older brothers attended and then donated.

Our house mandated that all brothers be a part of our meal plan. The meal plan was another way we kept the brotherhood strong. Every day at lunch and dinner, the house was buzzing with guys grabbing a bite, sharing stories, and making plans. Lifelong friendships were nurtured at the dinner table. I lived in the house for my entire college tenure. I liked living on campus and being where the action was. The house may have been falling apart, but it was our home. On any given afternoon, there were brothers studying, playing basketball, or hanging out. One of my favorite days was when someone purchased an inflatable pirate-ship kiddie pool, complete with inflatable pirate chest for our beer and an inflatable water cannon so we could hose down any scallywags who looked at us funny! To clarify, we did recruit some willing bikini-clad ladies to partake in our journey across the front lawn.

It is impossible to sum up what being a part of Greek society means to everyone. It is a personal experience that is not for everyone and not the same at every school. Like life, the system is at times flawed and unfair but also rewarding. Greek life can bring out the best in people and unlock hidden strengths; it is a uniquely collegiate experience that should not be overlooked.

Start Your Own Club or Organization

So you've been to the activities fair, and you've been back and forth between the student-activities office for the last week, and there still isn't a club or organization that fits what you're looking for. Well, then start one of your own. It's a challenge, to be sure, but it's a worthy one. Find a few people who share similar interests (or a culture or a religion) and find out what it takes to start your own club.

That's how the Latinos Club got started at Merrimack. Kendrys Vasquez and a few of his friends walked into the student-activities office and said they would like to start a Latinos club. "Super. Here's some money. Go start it. Let me know how it goes." They also got a lot of support from The Office of Diversity Education. (Actually, The Office of Diversity Education was salivating when it heard about the possibility of a Latinos club on our privileged white-boy campus.) And my goodness, you should have seen the events the club organized. People from schools all over Massachusetts were coming to the salsa parties and concerts that the Latinos Club hosted in the Merrimack student center. It was pretty crazy. I can't remember any other club having such an impact during my college days. And they were rewarded for their efforts, too. The Latinos Club got the Organization of the Year award. Grace Gatta, one of the senior advisors for the club, received the Unsung Hero Award, and Kendrys received the award for the most Outstanding Leader of the Class. Imagine if their idea to start the Latinos Club had died in conversation around their residence hall, as so many other ideas do (just for lack of initiative)?

This Is Your Legacy

Listen. Lest you think I'm running off at the mouth aimlessly about your involvement around campus, let's pause here for a moment so you can absorb what I'm talking about. *This is your opportunity to create your legacy at your school.* Maybe you'll get a 4.0 and graduate valedictorian of your class. Or maybe you're a star athlete and you get to sign autographs on your way across campus. Or maybe you are the lead vocal for a hot band, and everyone on campus is itching to get their hands on your latest song (and you). Awesome. But if you are one of the remaining 99.99 percent of the collegiate student body, what I'm offering you here is your very own opportunity to build your reputation, to leave your footprint. You want your professors and administrators talking about what a shame it is that you're graduating, that they wish every student could be like you. This is a very realistic goal, whether your school has forty thousand students or four thousand. It doesn't matter. You have your chance to leave your mark.

For me, at Merrimack, it was the Amazing Merrimack Race. As I said, I went to Merrimack to play basketball but had a tough go at making a name for myself on the court. During my senior year, my resident director, Jen, and I had a tradition of watching every episode of the CBS hit reality show *The Amazing Race*, where teams race around the world competing in different events. Several of us were in her apartment watching one Sunday evening, and Chris Kirwin, a fellow RA, turned to me during one of the commercials and said, "Dude, will you pass the bowl of jelly beans?" We really loved those jelly beans that Jen kept on her coffee table. I said, "Yes." And then he said, "Y'know, we really should consider bringing *The Amazing Race* to Merrimack." So we did. We campus-sized *The Amazing Race*. One sunny Saturday morning in April, we had seventy-three coed teams of two racing to complete eight preliminary events throughout campus, and the top ten teams got to compete in the final race for the top three prizes. We worked the final race in with a softball doubleheader and had a barbecue at the end. It was a blast.

The following year after I graduated, I came back and competed in The Amazing Merrimack Race as an alumnus. The same Amazing Merrimack Race that I had brought to campus. The same Amazing Merrimack Race that had etched my legacy at Merrimack. (And the same Amazing Merrimack

Race where I got bumped to third place because Twin Bob cheated. But I'm not bitter.)

Go to class so you can build a strong résumé for your future. Get involved on campus so you can leave your lasting impression on the college community—and have a great time in the process.

Politics

There are various stages of your life when you shape your "voice," and college is when that voice is really going to kick into high gear. More than likely, throughout your life, you've formulated opinions on who's cute and who's funny looking, which outfits are cool and which are hideous, who's funny and who's a dullard, which athlete is better than the next one, and on and on. Now that you're all "grown up," though, your interests are going to (or at least should) become more sophisticated. Idle gossip around the lunch table will be replaced by academic debates on the state of the economy or by which year was best for chardonnay bottled in eastern France. "Y'know, I'll tell ya, if you're just looking for the oaky aftertaste, I'd have to go with a 2004, but then, it also depends on what you're eating. If you're feasting on a delicate fish or seafood dish, like the seared ahi tuna I had last night, you'll want to lean away from heavily oak-influenced chardonnays and look at an older, mellower pairing or even an Italian blend with a dry white zin."

Or maybe politics tickle your fancy. You may have turned eighteen early in your senior year of high school and were fortunate enough to vote in an election. But even then, you might not have really taken the opportunity to get involved politically by participating in a rally or hanging up signs for your chosen candidate—or even getting to know the candidate's policy stances. Now that you've stepped foot on a college campus, you have the chance to make your political voice heard by getting involved and maybe even taking a stand. And just as with everything else in college, everybody (everybody!) starts on equal ground and everybody (everybody!) gets the opportunity to sound off. *Take advantage of your opportunity.* "How?" you ask.

Student-Government Association

I've got a good one for ya.

My friend Zack Wynne entered college in 2001 without a whole lot of friends. He was the self-proclaimed "fat kid at a beach college. I was sitting behind the eight ball from the beginning." But from day one, he got involved in politics on campus. He was not only looking to get involved in something, anything, but he really wanted to develop his understanding of the political world. "And, they give you free food at, like, every event," he told me. Fearing he'd lose if he ran for anything significant, he requested an open seat on the SGA. He went after it all year long—I'm talking really getting involved—and by the end of his freshman year, he was running for student-body president. He lost by a measly hundred votes his freshman year (aren't all elections lost by a measly hundred votes?) but won the next two elections and was even voted Homecoming King his senior year. *Homecoming King.* The fat kid at the beach college was voted Homecoming King. And then, after all that, during his first year of grad school, he was elected the president of the statewide association of student government. What the hell? I'm pretty sure he even had his own entourage opening doors for him and sweeping the ground in front of him and feeding him grapes one by one whenever he didn't feel like feeding himself.

Now, he's dropped sixty pounds, he looks amazing (so say the ladies), and most important, he has a fantastic network of colleagues in a field in which he's passionate. He has a stack of first-rate and very credible recommendation letters, and he's had the opportunity to meet bigwig political figures statewide. He even met Laura Bush when she came to campus. Life is pretty sweet for him right now, and it's interesting to think that he could have just been another number if he'd chosen not to get involved.

Get it? Regardless of your major, if you enjoy politics, or even if it's just an area in which you'd like to become more involved, student government can be a very worthy cause. And you can take it as far as you'd like (or not): you can be a class representative who just shows up for meetings to vote, or you can join the student senate or make a run at a cabinet position, like secretary or treasurer or even president. Understand that—depending on how high you rank—your involvement in SGA can be (and probably will be) your most rewarding and demanding collegiate experience, so either prepare yourself to go for it 100 percent or find something else that is more worthy of your efforts. This is your chance to really have your voice heard, but if you are not ready for the challenge, it's only fair to step aside for someone with the passion to take the platform. (Actually, in the interest of full disclosure, your involvement in SGA is something that you can probably half-ass—and get away with—just like so many other things in college, but that is not the legacy that you want to leave behind. Get involved in student government because you want to be the best representative that your school has ever had.)

Become a Club President

Outside the realm of academia, separating the below-average students from the average students from the above-average students is not hard to do. Below-average students don't do anything to get involved on campus: they go to class, and then they hole up in their rooms for an afternoon and evening of playing video games, watching movies, and studying. Pretty exciting. Average students get involved on campus in a club or organization or sorority or intramural sport or whatever.

And above-average students become club presidents.

If you're worried about the commitment it requires, don't be. Anybody who has some level of ambition can become a club president. In fact, the actual preparation *before* becoming president is probably more demanding than the act of being club president, since being the president is more about learning how to delegate duties than anything else. "You do this, and you organize that. I'm going out dancing." First, though, you're going to have to overachieve, as the grunt of the group, while you show those around you that you have what it takes—to not only accept responsibility, but to get twice the work done in half the time, and maybe with an innovative idea or two thrown in the mix. Volunteer to do the menial labor that no one else wants to tackle, and you're showing that you are serious about the club and that you can be held accountable for duties that your peers might not be able to handle. Then, when the time comes to cast votes, your fellow club members will know that you can be trusted to handle the important duties of president.

Beyond beefing up your résumé, earning respect, and making valuable connections, being a club president can do wonders for your confidence and focus in college. The sense of achievement that comes from being a successful authority figure on campus can balance out any rigorous academic schedule. Think about it. If you are all books, all the time, you're going to burn out, whereas the energy that you transfer by running a successful organization can get you excited to return to your residence hall for a late-night study session. And conversely, if you know that your college life is about more than just academics, you'll be able to relax and get more work done while looking forward to your club's activities.

Get involved in a club *now*, so you can become the club president *later*.

Stand Up for Something

If you're not convinced that the gratifying and valuable lifestyle of being a club president or joining SGA is for you, then you're probably right. But there are still plenty of options for you. One is to simply take a stand for something. Shoot man, this is your college, your country, your world, so make your voice heard. If something happens in your country or in your world or on your campus, you have a right to stand up and let your feelings be known. Write an editorial, stage a rally, pass out fliers, or march through the student union. Make it known that you—and your fellow students, whom you may or may not be able to muster up—have an opinion. Educate people. Tell them what you think and listen to what they have to say. No, you don't have to be a political leader or an incredible orator in order to attend a political rally. Just go! Make a difference! Care! It doesn't matter if you're an activist or a pacifist, a rightist or a leftist, a dentist or a florist . . . just let loose and let your "-ists" hang out. Today, political apathy is sweeping our college campuses. Don't be reluctant. Be aggressive! B-E aggressive! But be compassionate. If nothing else, you're going to feel a lot better after it's all over. We'll call it political therapy.

It's not enough anymore just to talk politics around the lunch table. Becoming politically involved allows you to become more aware of the world around you. When you vote, do you want to vote for the best-looking candidates and the ones with the coolest names, or do you want to be able to decipher the issues and determine who you think would be the best representative? It takes time to educate yourself and to determine your own political beliefs, so take that time now, while you're in college. Now is the time to experiment with different points of view!

Sports

Not everyone is a natural athlete. Not everyone has a chiseled frame or lightning quickness or a stellar jump shot. Fair enough. I get it. But not everyone who participates in sports— on some level—in college has a chiseled frame or lightning quickness or a stellar jump shot. As a matter of fact, college is filled with the most competitive nonathletes you'll ever meet in your life. Don't be shocked to hear the residence-hall walls speaking (or yelling) about a big intramural soccer game or a grudge match in tennis class.

Sports in college can be as serious or as casual as you want them to be. Maybe you want to join a physical education class just to stay in shape, or you want to form an intramural team in an effort to relive the glory days. Or maybe there's a coed team, and Bobby, with those beautiful brown eyes, asked you to play, and there's no way you can possibly say no. Great. No matter your motivation, getting involved in sports of some kind can complement the monotony of an otherwise-rigorous schedule of classes, club meetings, and research.

Physical Education Classes

Not all schools offer physical education classes. My college didn't, but many do, especially as the citizens of our fine nation grow wider and wider and as more importance is placed on physical fitness and health. So, if this is a core requirement at your institution—or if they're offered at all—don't discount these classes as slacker courses or extracurricular activities. Sure, that's what they are, but if you get serious, you can get a lot out of them, beyond just an hour or so of lollygagging around a few days per week. At North Carolina State, my friend Matt took a basketball class, and when I came home the summer after freshman year, he was setting backdoor screens off the ball and playing help defense. He even stole the ball from me once when I was driving to the hoop. It was clearly a foul (Yes, it was, hacker!), but the point is that he learned a lot about the game and he now knows a lot more than the kids in that class who just wanted a free period. (A couple of whom got Bs. In basketball class. How the hell do you get a B in basketball class?)

Not only can you use a phys ed class as an opportunity to stay in shape, but you can also learn about a sport or activity that you might end up enjoying for years to come. Either way, these are classes that you'll have to pay top-dollar for once you've graduated (often in the form of private lessons), so why not learn them now? I, for one, would have loved the chance to take a tennis course when I was an undergraduate, rather than suffering with a distorted backhand, a slow serve, and the inability to pick out a decent racquet, which could potentially solve both those issues.

Intramurals and Club Sports

In the movie *Teen Wolf*, Michael J. Fox is transformed from human to werewolf and becomes dominant on the basketball court. As his normal human self, he is a mediocre hoops talent at best—but when he becomes the wolf, nobody can stop him. He shoots, he scores, and afterward, he gets the girl.

My friends Dave and Brian Dlugasch are the perfect real-life examples of this. Outside the realm of competition, they are great guys: fun and studious—friends love them, teachers love them . . . everybody loves them. Then, they step on the field or court and they become werewolves: They start throwing their opposition around unapologetically and hollering at their teammates to dive on the ground rather than just watching the ball pass by. They get excited, they get angry, and afterward, they drag themselves back to their room to digest the evening's game and discuss how they can improve for the next game. It's about as intense as I've ever seen.

That's pretty much the definition of intramural and club sports. Normal, everyday weekend warriors metamorphose on the field or court to become an entirely different breed of athlete. It's pretty funny, actually. If you think you know somebody, double-check on the intramural playing field for a second opinion.

Your school will have a wide variety of intramural sports available and, depending on the level of interest, will probably have different levels to sign up for. So you'll have the option to play at the top level with top talent or to just play for fun with a few friends who just want to get out and get some exercise (although, even then, you're likely to come across some pretty hostile adversaries). In either event, this is a great way to gather a group of friends from your residence hall or throughout campus (or sign up solo through the office of student activities) to compete against your peers. It's fun (I've seen rivalries carry from season to season through all four years) and healthy (you'll be able to stay in shape and, at the very least, curb that wicked Freshman Fifteen) and a great opportunity to add even more range to your already-dynamic lifestyle. And the ladies dig intramural champions.

Club sports often fill a void when a particular sport isn't offered at the varsity level. Generally, these might be less visible sports, like fencing or rugby or Ultimate Frisbee, although some schools offer major sports as a supplement to the varsity athletics that are already offered. Club sports can be a great way to compete with other schools or community teams at a level higher than that of intramurals but without the demand that varsity athletics can bring. Coaches often frown upon a missed practice at the varsity level, while club sports don't require the same level of commitment (but can still be just as much fun). Check to see which club sports are available at your school, or if you can generate enough interest, start your own team. Be warned, however, that club sports are infrequently funded by a school, so prepare yourself for hefty travel and equipment expenses, which can accumulate quickly.

Varsity Athletics

Those who compete at the varsity level in college can count themselves among the lucky. For whatever reason—lack of talent or circumstance—a lot of sports dreams die after high school, but if you intend to play a varsity sport in college, there are several things to keep in mind.

First, competing at a varsity level means that everything else in your life needs to be scaled down to size. Since you're looking at a serious year-round commitment, you will have a difficult time getting heavily involved in organizations—as a club president, for example, your summer or winter or spring breaks might be cut short by a lengthy athletic season, and while your friends are studying abroad for a semester or a year, you'll have to scale back to a month during the summer. Most important, you will have to manage your time better than your peers who are not playing sports, since academic commitments can often become cumbersome alongside off-season training sessions, practices, and games.

Second, college varsity athletics are (obviously) more intense than any competitive venture you've ever undertaken. So be prepared. Nobody cares that you were the star of your high school team; every college athlete was the star of their high school team. Your coach may feign playing favorites, but if you've got your opportunity to play on a varsity athletic team, you've got your shot—just like the next guy—of showing your capabilities. Don't waste it.

Finally, competing on a varsity level requires a commitment beyond just time. Your life is under the microscope now, so you must act responsibly. If you get caught drinking underage or smoking marijuana in the quad (really?) or if your grades start to fall off, you better believe your coach's office is on most administrators' speed dial. With the glory of being in the spotlight also comes accountability, so be prepared to act maturely enough to handle it.

All that said, my experience playing college basketball was about the most rewarding experience of my life. Even despite a subpar career, I'm grateful for the opportunity that I had to compete at that level and for the great people I was able to meet along the way. My life—from volunteerism to academics—was guided by my decision to play basketball, and it's one of the best decisions I've ever made.

Spectator Events

Whether you are an aficionado of sport or you don't particularly care who wins or loses, it's important (and fun!) to show support for your school's athletic programs by attending as a spectator. These are guys and gals who have spent thousands of hours honing their skills in an effort to impress you, the fan, so it's only fair (and fun!) that you give them encouragement by showing up to cheer them on . . . with your face painted the school colors. Besides, sporting events are generally very entertaining, and even better, as a student, you'll probably get priority seating for free. Can't beat that.

Don't discount less popular sports. Rather than going to basketball or football games every week, make your way out to field hockey or lacrosse games. If a team continues to lose, though, maybe they just haven't worked hard enough to deserve your support, so wait until they start winning again to hop back on the bandwagon. Or just pick another sport that is winning. There are a thousand other things you could be doing instead, so being a fair-weather fan is most absolutely acceptable.

Mixing Academics with Extracurricular Activities

Beyond an assistantship with a professor or writing a research report on the history of your favorite band (an assignment you shouldn't anticipate receiving), it is very possible to bridge the gap between business and pleasure in college. As a matter of fact, it's important to make the connection, for fear that all your exams and research papers and readings start running together.

I have three ideas here, although you're sure to discover more after you set foot on campus. My primo advice? You guessed it: take advantage of (almost) every opportunity thrown your way.

Study Abroad

I've mentioned it several times before, and I'll talk about it again right now (and probably a few more times before this book's over with): Go abroad. Go abroad; go abroad; go abroad. *Go abroad!* Get the hell out of this country. Really. There is no question that America is the greatest country on the planet—in nearly every aspect—but college is a great time for you to expand your horizons by expanding your comfort zone.

Maybe you are able to go away for a year or a semester or, if you're too heavily leveraged in other activities around campus, just a summer. But it doesn't matter. And please consider going to a country that doesn't speak English. My goodness. I (and maybe this is a unique opinion) consider it a mistake when students go abroad to Canada or England or Australia. Even Ireland—where they speak some sort of indecipherable English that no one can really understand—doesn't count. Don't you want to get the full experience? Go to France or China or Ecuador. Work on learning a new language, a new culture. You don't have to take classes in French or Chinese or Spanish unless you want to, but you can pick up a few phrases along the way, and you can learn about native cooking or music or dance. Australia is a great country, and you've got the rest of your life to get there for surfing and snorkeling, but you don't have the rest of your life to study abroad.

The best part of studying abroad is the people you will meet. Once you've graduated and you become a world traveler, it isn't as easy to connect with people in the countries to which you travel, but through a study abroad program, you've already got a collection of fellow students waiting for you. This is especially true in foreign countries where they are much more welcoming of international students than we are here in the United States (perhaps because they are totally fascinated by how ignorant we are of world affairs or because everyone in America is an immigrant already).

I had two great experiences studying abroad while I was in college. I spent a summer in Seville, Spain, living with the most adorable old lady named Margarita. And then I spent a summer in San Miguel de Allende, Mexico, studying in one of Mexico's premiere language schools. Just like I've hinted, it exceeded the cultural experience I had been expecting. I met some of the most fantastic people (some of whom I still keep in contact with today), and I visited landmarks that you can't possibly appreciate through travel books. Beyond the priceless cultural experience, the credits I earned abroad were far, far less expensive than the courses at Merrimack. Muahahahaha. Suckers.

Go to Guest Lectures

I don't care who your teachers are or which school you've chosen to attend, you can't possibly learn everything in the classroom. You can learn *a lot* within academic halls, but the key to a universal education is to broaden your scope, to get out there and learn from the world around you. Read books and magazines and periodicals; talk to people; join organizations. And go to guest lectures.

The size and budget of your school might determine the level of celebrity they're able to attract, but *every* school has the capability to bring an assortment of authors or politicians or scientists to campus. In some cases these guest lectures will be short on intrigue and long on monotony, but then there will be that one lightbulb moment where you are motivated to take action. In many cases, these guest lectures will be both informative and inspirational as you sit back to hear the tales on how these famous people were able to reach their level of success. And as a bonus, your professors will love the idea that you are putting in the effort to attend these guest lectures. Oh, what sophistication!

Work on Something Big

Part of graduating with a smile on your face involves more than merely evaluating your potential now that you have a diploma in your hand. Taking a moment to look back at your accomplishments since Mommy and Daddy dropped you off at orientation, did you do anything *big*? You graduated with a solid GPA, you joined a couple of organizations, you won an intramural football championship, and you received recognition for your volunteer work. But that's it?

No matter what you do, include a major project in the mix, something that you work on from start to finish, beginning with your freshman year. I can't tell you what that project might be. Consider what you're good at (remember "specializing" in chapter 4?), what you love, and what you're after. Maybe you are a writer or you want to improve your writing, so you can work on writing your own book. Or maybe you start a band and your goal is to cut a CD and sell a few while you tour the state. Maybe you see a need to establish a volunteer organization that links much-needed mentors with the poor, uneducated children of a local town. Hell, the possibilities are literally endless. Just think of something, and get going on it.

> The very best students are separated by the size of their accomplishments. Think big; perform big. At the very least, it can only add to your résumé while sharpening a skill set that you can use for the rest of your life, and at best, it can be an ambitious undertaking that keeps you energized throughout your college years. And who knows where it could lead? Many businesses that began in college residence halls, for example, became lifelong pursuits for some of today's most successful entrepreneurs.

Chapter in Brief

Okey dokey, let's review:

- Do research and get involved—your first two weeks—in a club or organization on campus, whether it be religious, cultural, service oriented, a fraternity or sorority, or something you start yourself.
- Whether you're passionate or not, involve yourself in the political community. Join SGA, become a club president, or attend a rally. Learn your politics.

- From intramurals to club to varsity, there is a college sport with your name on it.
- Mixing extracurricular activities with your academic life is fun and educational.
- Complete a major project before you graduate.

SEVEN

Break Time!

M mm, break time. Welcome to heaven! You've been working hard all semester, and now you get the opportunity to return home to unwind. Or maybe you'll jet off to some exotic location for a little R&R. Good times await, for sure.

Breaks from school are most definitely an ideal time to recline and collect yourself after a stretch of grueling courses. You've earned it! Break time, though, can also be an ideal opportunity to rejuvenate and prepare for the upcoming term. Since it is very possible for you to become lackadaisical (and thus return to school rusty and ill prepared to get back in the groove of being a student), how can you maximize—and balance—both fun and productivity in the wake of the temptation to waste away on the couch? Should you study during the break? Work? Or just relax? And do you have to spend money you don't have just to get out of Dodge? Ahh! All these stressful questions, and break time is supposed to be leisurely, isn't it? Of course, but you want to *carpe quasso*—seize the break—and here's how.

Short Breaks

No matter what, things only get better, so keep in mind that, however much trouble you're having fighting through classes, there is a break right around the corner. Embrace that concept, and use it as motivation to keep going just a little longer because, after you graduate, odds are that you'll have less freedom (certainly less time) to escape the realities of your life.

Shorter breaks are unique—obviously—from your longer summer vacation in that you won't really have time to find a groove, or if you do, it will be time to return to school just as soon as you do. Be prepared to answer inquiries about your holiday experiences with, "*Ugh,* I had so much fun. I did [this and that], but breaks are never long enough. Just as I was starting to get used to it, I had to start packing to come back to school." It's inevitable that breaks will always be a week too short, but that doesn't mean you can't have a fabulous time while you're away from the academic grind.

Do Not Spend Your Break Vegging Out

Spring, winter, and fall breaks might not necessarily provide enough time to organize any kind of routine, like returning to your old job, but there is still plenty to do beyond settling for the "same old, same old" activities that your friends from high school are involved in. Gathering at a friend's house for a reunion is fun for a night, but returning to the same bar night after night for a week will become dangerously monotonous. And if you spend all your free time at home in front of the TV (because "you earned this time to yourself"), you'll miss out on lots of opportunities around you.

Maybe you can return to your old job (which you should

have arranged while you were home for Thanksgiving—they can use your experience and flexible hours over the *winter break*), but no matter what, you can definitely take the time to hustle up some money in your neighborhood by doing odd jobs for a few hours a day. Cutting grass, shoveling snow, babysitting, or any other job you can think of can be vital to your bank account, since instead of spending money, you'll be earning it. A month's worth of scanty paychecks can fund your social expenses for a semester or pay for your next spring-break trip. It's perfectly fine—and important—to relax while you're home on leave from academics. But balance that relaxation with some sort of productivity.

Take Short Trips

Break time was fun for me in college because it gave me the opportunity to get out of town and visit places I had been learning about in class. It's fun to hear about the art at the Louvre in Paris, but it's a whole different experience to actually see it right there staring back at you. And since Spanish was one of my majors in college, I took short trips to the south of Spain and the backcountry of Mexico to live an adventure that you just can't have by listening to a professor's lecture. Trips out of the country can become costly, though, and those trips might actually be better if planned for longer periods of time, since your main expense is your plane ticket. Indeed, I had just about as much fun abroad as I did going to New York City to play tourist (complete with I ♥ NY shirt and camera strapped around my neck).

In general, I recommend short trips as opposed to longer trips that might take up your whole break, because it's important to balance leisure with your other responsibilities. Maybe you have a few assignments to work on while you're on hiatus or you need to hustle up a few dollars by working (rather than putting everything on the Visa). Good. Don't ignore the fact that you can have fun and take care of other necessities in the process. Short trips allow you to see what you want to see and then return home to get back to business. It's fun to spend your entire spring vacation bronzing your skin on the beaches of Daytona, but don't get lost loafing around when you could have a spring break that you'll really remember—say, by visiting a destination with some kind of historic or cultural significance.

> Oh yeah! Hot tip alert: Break time is a *fantastic* time to visit your friends who live out of town. You can travel somewhere you've never been, and this comes with the added bonus of a free place to stay and a built-in social agenda waiting for you upon arrival. And besides, most moms' home cooking is just as good as—if not better than—any food you'll find on your travels (and the price is right, too).

Budgeting Your Trips

For many students, break time can be just as stressful as time spent at school, for the lone reason that costs can add up quickly. Some of my friends were reckless with their spending habits in college, some were overly thrifty, and others were simply smart with their money. The last group, the ones who didn't stress but also didn't spend extravagantly, were the ones who got the most out of the trips that they organized because they were fun and economical.

Beyond visiting friends for *every* break, there are plenty of ways to save a buck on destination trips. If you're into five-star treatment, I don't know what to tell you, but why not go camping once in a while? Outdoor activities are the most fun, and these kind of trips are cheap and beautiful. Also, keep your eye out—always—for package deals where a company will bundle airfare with hotel accommodations and maybe even food and drink. Investigate these deals and get referrals, because some of the deals that appear too good to be true are, indeed, too good to be true. A solid package by a reputable company can both save you money and send you to a destination with other college students from around the country (if you're looking to tread the beaten path).

Of course, depending on the trip, you're likely to want to travel with a group of friends, so keep your eye out for group deals or maybe even try to set up a group deal of your own. My favorite ski trip, to Copper Mountain in Colorado, involved fifteen guys in a luxurious three-bedroom condo. We paid seventy-seven dollars each for the accommodations, and we certainly didn't care that most of us had to sleep in sleeping bags or on air mattresses. After all, we were there to spend our time *outside* the condo, on the ski slopes, anyway. We also saved big by cooking quantity meals with bulk ingredients (John Graham's Swiss Chicken Surprise cost us $2.43 per head) and stuffing ourselves inside rental cars like clowns at a circus. No kidding, it was probably the best trip I've ever been on, and it was super cheap.

In any event, start planning your trips as soon as possible. Spontaneous trips in college are a blast, but they can also be costly, whereas a trip planned well in advance can keep lots of dough in your pocket. The closer you delay until trip time, the more likely airfare and accommodations will rise in price—if they are even still available.

Be Responsible

Maybe you go to school in a warmer climate and you desire to head north for a ski vacation. Or maybe you've spent all this time in the north and it's time for you to get to the beach. No matter your destination, I've said it once and I'll say it again: you are an adult now! Just because you see kids going nuts on TV (*Girls Gone Wild,* anyone?) doesn't mean that every single college kid in America is irresponsible with their vacation time. Some are, of course, but that doesn't mean you have to be an idiot right along with them. Golly, man . . . you do understand that you can have fun and be responsible with your life, too, don't you? Besides, how much fun is it to come home with an STI, a headache, and an extra five pounds of beer weight? Those are stories that I've heard all too often.

No matter what you do, *call your parents.* Your parents are already worried, so be sure to keep the lines of communication open by calling them once in a while. "Mama's boy?" Damn right, be a mama's boy. You wouldn't be here without them, and it's only fair that you share these experiences. Listen. Your parents have been there. I don't care how geeky or innocent your parents may appear, they were immature tykes once, and they know what's running through your head when you get vacation time. And that's why they're worried about you. So, isn't it fair that you ease their minds a little by opening up and letting them know you're okay? Besides, if your parents are in the loop, it makes life a lot easier for you when it's time to start asking for favors.

Go Places That Aren't Normal

The most fun cultural destinations—to us Americans, anyway—seem to be out of the country, although it's certainly true that there is plenty of history right here on American soil. My recommendation is to take advantage of any opportunity you have to get the hell away from the crowds and onto a path where you can create your own journey. "Where'd you go during the break?" Costa Rica. I swam with dolphins, zip-lined through the jungle, took a weeklong cooking class, and met some lovely Latin ladies, who showed me a dance move or two. Where'd you go? "Oh . . . uh . . . well . . . uh . . . Myrtle Beach. I . . . uh . . . judged a wet T-shirt contest."

Have you ever been to Gettysburg or Kitty Hawk or a winery in northern California? Take this as an opportunity to explore your interests. More fun is had on America's back roads than anywhere else. Think about it. How cool would it be to make contact with a cattle farmer in Texas who might let you come to his ranch to herd and lasso steers for a week? Or maybe you could locate a shrimp boat that would let you work in exchange for a portion of the catch. Random, sure, but it might be the most fun you ever have, and you won't be anywhere near half-naked boys or girls and glistening beaches. Take this as a chance to explore what piques your interest. You live only once, and one wasted vacation after another can add up.

Embrace Alternative Spring Break Opportunities

Now, you're talking. How would you like to have the experience of a lifetime *and* make a difference in the life of someone less fortunate than you? (Yes, your life is fortunate. Sure you've faced adversity and tough times, but so has everybody else, and here you are, in college. Many people don't have that opportunity, homes, so consider yourself fortunate.) Alternative Spring Break, if it is offered by your school, is a fantastic way to do something that few others are doing, to see a side of life that few of your peers get to see, and best of all, to help people in need. It's definitely worth doing for at least one of your four years in college. The beaches will be there forever, but the people you can help need that help *now*.

Best of all, with most Alternative Spring Break trips, you can find sponsors and hold fund-raisers and end up having your trip paid for by someone else. How cool is that? Make a difference for free! Very cool. And I promise you—an ASB trip is not one that you will soon forget. You'll meet people—good people who won't give you herpes—whom you might keep in touch with for the rest of your life. And to see the smiles on people's faces—the helpers and the helped—is priceless.

If your school doesn't have ASB, start it. It's not that difficult—much easier than starting a club or organization. Just get the appropriate sponsorship and then start baking cookies or whatever it is you decide to do to raise money.

Summer Break

Summer break allows for a lot more freedom than a shorter winter, spring, or fall break, but with that freedom comes responsibility—and you can waste away valuable time just as easily as you can seize these precious months. Every college student looks forward to (nay, *yearns for*) the lengthy summer break, but very few understand how to make the most of it, and even those who do usually figure it out too late. *Start planning your summer break in January.*

Most of the tactics I've spoken about already can apply to summer break. Summer is a great time to take short trips (as discussed above), especially to visit your friends who live in other cities. And studying abroad—as discussed in chapter 6—if it can't be fit into the school year, can work in nicely during the summer. After all, many language schools claim (and it's true) that you can achieve proficiency in a language by spending just three months fully immersed in it, which makes summertime an ideal time to hightail it out of the country.

But how else should you be spending your summer months? Should you work? Study? Take courses? And if so, how do you go about balancing the leisure and work of your longest hiatus from school—a time when you should be relaxing and enjoying your precious free moments?

Work and Save

It might be questionable whether you can return to your old job—or some job—during your winter break, but there is no question you need to be working—in some capacity—during the summer. After all, there are several factors at play here. First, you don't want to spend the summer months being completely lazy and getting so soft that you'll return to school rusty and ill prepared to get back into the working mind-set. Also, *you need money.* You need money during the summer, and you need to save money for the school year, and summer break is the best time to "stack paper" (shout out to my boys back at the moving company in Charleston for hooking me up with all of the cool slang terms found throughout *The Best Four Years*). The more money you can accrue during the summer, the less you'll have to work—and worry—during the school year. This is a great time to really mind the advice from chapter 3: be smart with your money. Geez. How many times have I seen my friends go crawling to Mommy and Daddy midsemester, asking for money, since they didn't take the time to write out a simple budget? You don't want this to happen to you, for two reasons: 1.) You are trying to show your parents—and everyone else around you—how responsible and grown up you are, so you don't want to get in the habit of asking them to bail you out; and 2.) You would like to hope they'll be there when you *really* need them and not just when you're being stupid with your money. Habitually asking them for help can compromise that relationship.

The summer after my freshman year, I came home from school, and the only hours I could get at my old job—waiting tables at Bob Evans Restaurant—were on Saturday and Sunday. Well, clearly that wasn't going to get me ahead of the game or out of my mom's hair during the week. So, I drafted a flier that I distributed throughout my side of town offering my fifteen-dollar-an-hour services for—well, anything. Need somebody to cut your grass? Give me a call. Brush removal? I'm your guy. Walk the dog? Stain the deck? Massage your feet? Read bedtime stories? I'll do it all. I had so much work that summer, it was unbelievable. Doc Stephenson contracted me for a hundred hours. Bud Batts took me on the truck to do landscaping with him for twenty or so days that summer. It was fantastic. Best of all, I got to make my own hours. And since people came to trust my work, I didn't have to deal with a fire-breathing boss staring down at me all day long. They just gave me a list and left me to it.

If you're going to get really ambitious on me, summer is a good time to start working on that internship I've mentioned several times already. Whether you get paid or not, a summer internship allows you to put into practice all the principles and knowledge you have been developing for these last two (or four or six) semesters. After all, if you're book-smart and book-smart only, you'll be worthless to potential future employers. They don't want robots. They want people who have experience getting their hands dirty in the real world. Employers want to hire you and set you free to work, rather than having to coddle you through the training process. An internship—whether it is a paid gig as a copy editor at your local paper, or you're offering your time for free shadowing an expert in your chosen field—puts you well ahead of your peers who are returning to the same dead-end summer jobs.

If you do continue to return to the same dead-end job in the summer, ask for more responsibility each time. Sell yourself to your manager as having become a better employee while away at college and let them know that you are ready for more. This will earn you more respect (and, I hope, more money), and it will also allow you the opportunity to pad your résumé.

Take a Course or Two (or Three or Four)

You're going to hate yourself if you spend your summer sleeping in late every day, watching DVDs, and experimenting with different concoctions on the stove. Trust me—not only will you waste away, but your self-esteem will nosedive. Your friends will start neglecting you, and tensions will rise around the house as your mom swears if you don't get yourself off the couch, she'll get you off the couch herself.

One terrific way to break that monotony is to take a couple courses. I never took summer classes, and now I look back on it as one of the more major mistakes I made in college. Ah, regret. There's plenty of time for regret in college, but you don't want it to be in the academic arena.

Taking courses in the summer allows you to focus on a tougher or boring course that you don't want to take in the mix with the rest of your courses throughout the school year. I can think of several courses (Philosophy!) that I would have loved to have isolated and focused on in the summer, rather than trudging through along with the rest of my challenging course load.

Plus, taking courses in the summer eases the work you have to do during the year (and can even shed a semester or a year off of your college career—if you're on a fast track to bigger and better things in your life). If you take two classes in the summer, that's one fewer class you have to take each semester. Pretty sweet. If you take two per session, you can really slack off during the school year. More than that, you're all but guaranteed an A if you put in the effort, for a couple of reasons. First, you have more time to devote to the course, so instead of devoting ten hours to studying for five courses, you have all this time to focus on just one or two. Second (and most important!), professors tend to be more lenient and sympathetic during the summer than they are during the school year. Generally, their minds are elsewhere during the summer—working on a research project or a book—and *not* in the classroom. They are not at all concerned with the fact that they have to cram a sixteen-week course into six or twelve weeks. They just want to get it over with, and this will work to your benefit.

It took me a while, but now I understand how some of the most scatterbrained athletes on my college campus were staying eligible: they took summer courses. And it was a very smart play on their part.

Keep Your Mind Sharp

Even if it doesn't work out for you to take courses over the summer—because you already have so much going on—it is critical that you keep your mind sharp. Again, you don't want to get rusty and have to spend the first two weeks of school (a very valuable two weeks) getting back on track. A healthy mind breeds a healthy spirit, and a healthy spirit transfers from one area of your life to another. Really. Sounds corny, but it's true.

Keeping your mind sharp is simple. Read. Write. Watch *Jeopardy*. From writing in your journal for fifteen minutes a day to keeping a book handy wherever you go, don't neglect the need for cognitive stimulation. Maybe you can get by during spring or winter without sharpening your mind (though I wouldn't risk it), but the summer break is just too long for a mental lapse. Plus, you never know when inspiration may choose to strike. If you're not exercising the analytical functions of your brain, you're not fueling your creativity, and you risk blocking a great idea for a writing competition in the fall, or a research project, or a business plan—ideas that might not strike you when you return to the classroom. As school lets out for the summer, your thoughts are free to extend beyond the mechanics of textbooks, so allow your mind to stay sharp, focused, and free.

Relax Already!

All this talk about working and taking courses and taking quick trips has me exhausted, and that certainly contradicts the idea behind break time. The fact is that college is intense, and breaks are strategically placed to allow you to relax, to ease your mind from the biting pressure that academics can bring. So while it's important to keep your mind sharp and avoid becoming lazy during your time off, it's also important to recognize that you've worked hard hitting the books, and now is a time to rejuvenate before diving in again. Enjoy this time! Take time to sit back and relax. Reunite with family and friends. Do the fun things you've been putting off for so long because the timing wasn't convenient. Now's the time! Shoot, you've earned this free time, and trust me, before you know it, you'll be right back at it. *Don't burn yourself out,* but stay sharp.

Chapter in Brief

Okey dokey, let's review:

- Break time is your opportunity to relax and rejuvenate, so use this time as such. *But don't waste away on the couch.* Embrace opportunities in front of you.
- Be responsible, especially on spring break. Just

because everybody else is being an idiot doesn't
mean you have to be.

- Go to work and save money for the school year; take
  short trips and see places you've only read about; or
  take a few courses and get ahead for the school year.
  Keep your mind sharp!

- I repeat . . . break time is your opportunity to relax
  and rejuvenate, so use this time as such. Don't burn
  yourself out!

EIGHT

A Social Affair

Short (barely) of hearing about the birds and the bees, you're probably going to get a serious talking-to from your parents about the ills and thrills of college's social scene. And if you're in for a sixteen-hour trip up the East Coast with Daddy, I hope you packed sleeping pills. After all, what do your parents know, right? They're old and gray. They don't have a clue! "Yeah yeah, Ma. I get it. 'Don't drink and drive.' 'Wear a condom.' 'And don't accept candy from strangers.' I'm all over it."

Truth is that there's a lot of merit to your parents' advice—with the caveat that times are clearly different with every generation, and most notably, social networks on the Internet make this a completely different ballgame today than when your parents were young. Your parents know—and have probably seen firsthand—the repercussions of being irresponsible, and they don't want to see you taint the masterpiece that they've spent the last eighteen years constructing. Your best interests are most certainly in the hearts of your parents, so heed their advice.

And also heed mine in these next few pages. Handling your academic life is cake compared with the challenge of meeting the right people and doing the right things in college. After all, the secret to academics is pretty cut-and-dried—get your nose in the books—but your social life is more learn-as-you-go, which is a lot scarier. That said, the best (and most successful) students are able to balance study time with party time, while those who lean heavily one way or the other rarely get the most out of college. Here—handling your social life with grace—is how you can look back years after graduation and proclaim, "I wouldn't change a thing!"

Meeting People

If there's one thing I did absolutely right in college, it was connecting with good people. Actually, looking back, it's the lone skill that I've mastered over the years: surrounding myself with people who are going places. It's not that I'm funnier or better looking or more sophisticated than the next person; I just have a knack for connecting with respectable folks. Really. I have some of the best friends around, and I foster those friendships because they are important to me. And if they aren't, then I let them go. "Just saying no" is harder than it sounds, but I've had plenty of practice, and by the time I was through with college, I was a specialist at shedding the negative influences and people in my life and embracing the positive ones.

Make your friends a priority. No doubt about it. These are the people whom you'll socialize with on the weekends, study with during the week, and lean on for sympathetic ears when times are tough. You *need* good friends, but more important, good friends help shape you into the person you're destined to become. If your clique comprises assholes, then you're more apt to become an asshole. If you're clique comprises wholesome, good-natured characters, then you'll be wholesome and good-natured yourself. It's pretty simple, actually. But where do you go to meet these fantastic people whom you want to call your friends?

Meet Your RA First

If there's one person who's "been there, done that," it's your RA. Maybe they haven't seen it all, but they were freshmen once, so their college experience trumps yours, and they want to help you have the best year of your life.

RAs range in personality and taste and wisdom, from one end of the spectrum to the other. Some are social and some are nerds; some are extroverts and some are introverts. They're all different, which is how it should be. There's no mold for an RA, and that will work to your advantage as you use them as one of your social resources. Connect with them to find out where to get involved on campus, where to sit in the cafeteria, where to party, and where to avoid. Even if they are the geekiest of the geeks, they have eyes and ears and they know what's going on. When they have programs in your hall, *go to them*. You'll put a smile on their face, you'll have fun, and you'll meet your neighbors (the important ones, rather than the slackers holed up in their rooms). Later, once you've developed a relationship with your RA, you can offer suggestions of your own for activities or off-campus outings. They generally have a budget to spend, so help them spend it.

Too many people see their RAs as the "bad guys," and that just isn't the case. Sure, they are there to enforce the rules—noise violations, vandalism, out-of-control alcohol abusers—but they don't like writing people up any more than people like getting written up. It's the tough part of the job, so be on your best behavior. Your RA might be your first friend and your inside connection to what's hip around campus, so don't compromise that relationship by acting foolish.

Get Involved and Meet Like-Minded People

As I discussed in more detail in chapter 6, getting involved in campus activities can make or break your college experience. Most assuredly, your involvement on campus can establish your reputation, but this is also where you can meet people with interests and attitudes similar to your own. Of course, you want to build a diverse circle of friends—a group of all the same personality can get old quick—but campus involvement provides an icebreaker whether you are outgoing or not. Begin your friend search in the Asian club or in a fraternity or at a meeting of the National Association for the Advancement of Little People, and branch out from there. Read posters and attend every social function that looks appealing to you. Go to movies, concerts, or other shows on campus. And don't be afraid to go by yourself. Cliques are established early in college (sad, but true), but solid friendships take time to cultivate, so don't feel like you missed the boat just because you haven't met the right people quite yet.

Surround Yourself With Positivity

Getting involved in campus activities also gives you a head start on surrounding yourself with positive people. *This should be your top priority in college.* Well, maybe second to your education, but it's a close second. We'll call it a tie. Listen—if you spend your time associating with people who inspire negativity or love drama, it's going to usurp your already-limited supply of energy. Here you are, running all over campus with all these activities and studying for exams and writing papers, and now you have to deal with your friends complaining about the most ridiculous little issues you could possibly imagine? It could be your downfall. Really. High school drama has nothing on college drama. You'll see.

Surrounding yourself with positivity can only help your achievement in and out of the classroom. If you're associated with top performers, then you're more likely to be a top performer yourself. If your friends have positive attitudes, then you're more likely to carry forward that same spirit from one area of your life to another. You want optimum achievement, and the people you choose to have as your friends can make that difference. Cut the deadweight.

> For me, it was never difficult to cut the deadweight. If someone had a negative influence on me, I dispatched them out from my life rather quickly. It's not difficult. Talk about a socially capitalistic society: college is loaded with good people and bad, and the great thing for you is that you have plenty of people from whom to choose your friends. Foster healthy friendships and dispel the bad ones. If somebody has an adverse influence on you, move on to someone who will appreciate the positive aura that you bring to the world. And hold on to their friendship for dear life. It's that easy.

Your Room, Your Residence Hall, Your Campus

Even the most introverted person can't get through college without meeting people. They're everywhere; your school is an open field, and you have the freedom to spread your seed wherever you'd like. Okay, that's a pretty horrible metaphor, but you get the idea: there are lots of opportunity for you to meet people.

Beyond forming a friendship with your roommate (or at least a truce; my goodness, that's one person with whom you do not want to bump heads), if you keep your door open, you're setting off the vibe that you are open to making new friends. Someone may spot a movie poster on your wall or be intrigued by the way you have your room set up, and they'll stop by just to say hi. Indeed, you'll want to keep your door closed when you're on the phone or doing schoolwork or making out with Betty Sue, but you don't want to miss the opportunity to meet your neighbors passing by.

The halls beyond your hallway are grounds for meeting even more people. Whether it's in the residence-hall lounge or game room (or if you want to be creepy, walk up to all the open doors and just start talking to people), there are plenty of opportunities to shake hands and exchange a laugh right there in your living quarters. The point is that the more you are out and about—even if you're a nervous Nellie and you don't like talking to people—the more chances you have to interact with your peers.

The further you cast your social net, the greater your odds are of accumulating a diverse set of interesting acquaintances. By broadening your search to the entire campus, you can meet upperclassmen and underclassmen alike, but you can also meet people with a wide range of interests. It's amazing how many people you can meet in the weight room or the game room at the student center or at the snack bar next to the cafeteria. Ask to join someone for lunch. Hustle up a game of pool or Ping-Pong. Once you've broken the ice with someone, it makes it so much easier to flare up a conversation the next time you see them.

Go Out and Find Fun (or Boredom Will Find You)

You can't just hang around and wait for good times to come. Sure, it's college, but it isn't that easy. You have to put in a little effort here.

The trick to good times is to never lose your sense of adventure. I say this isn't easy, because, starting with your freshman year and continuing through your senior year, responsibilities and distractions will continue to mount. Freshman year, although challenging for sure, is easier because it's all still fresh and new and you're getting your land legs under you, discovering your surroundings. Then sophomore year hits, and it isn't as easy as it once was. Now you have a tougher course load. And a boyfriend. And a job. And you are the vice president of The League of Women with Moles on the Lower Back. And . . . and . . . and . . . with all this new responsibility, you start to lose that sense of adventure that is so important.

Spontaneity is a virtue, and your master key to good times. Get out there! Dress up for a theme party or throw one of your own; hop in the car for a random weekend road trip; play tourist in your own town and visit those places that you swear you'll get to "sooner or later"; ask Susie out to a play, even though your friends swear you don't have a chance in

> hell. Take some risks here, babe. Balancing academics and
> social life becomes more of a challenge—and requires more
> creative thought on your part—as time passes, so start build-
> ing that creative muscle right now.

It's important, though, to understand that you're not trying to create a string of morning-after what-an-idiot-I-am-for-doing-that-type stories (although one or two of those shouldn't hurt too bad). On the contrary, you're looking for a series of yeah-I-did-that accomplishments. Let loose, but don't be irresponsible. Take a chance, but leave yourself an out. Have fun, not regret. Despite what you may have heard, fun and regret can act independently of each other, and you don't want to find that out the hard way.

Friends Won't Always Hang Around

College doesn't bring anything new to the idea that the friends you have today might not be around tomorrow or next week or next semester. You already know about the possibility that friends—good friends, even—can grow apart. Which is cool. It happens. It's not you. It just is. And that idea becomes even more pronounced in college, as you throw in other complexities: You lived next to Bart freshman year, but then he moved across campus sophomore year; you and Francesca were undeclared majors early on, but once she declared, she started hanging out with her fellow engineers; you thought you had a lot in common with Marjorie, but then she got fourteen piercings and started wearing black lipstick. And on and on. Dynamics change, and people change—sometimes for better, sometimes for worse. Don't get your drawers all bunched up about it.

There is one caveat that I've already mentioned briefly, and I'll stress it here: *foster the friendships that you consider important.* It's one thing for you to simply grow apart from someone you thought would turn out to be a good friend, but it's completely different for you to neglect an otherwise-great friendship. Close friendships, just like any other worthy pursuit in life, require work. You can't expect that just because you call someone your best friend and you have them as speed-dial number one on your phone (ahead of voice mail!), that they actually be your best friend. No way. It takes time and effort. They need a high five when they're up, a helping hand when they're down, and you by their side when things are normal. And it must be genuine. Close friends can read right through your BS when you lean in for a counterfeit hug and tell them, "Aw, everything's gonna be okay, Sweetie." Bring the same passion and authenticity to the table as you would with any other noble undertaking. They deserve it, and so do you.

I'm not trying to lay down the law about how you should make friends. That's up to you, and everybody has their own personality. I'm just saying that, in the midst of gaining and losing friends throughout your college career, you should make friends with two or three really great people—people you'd do anything for—and do everything you can to hold onto those priceless friendships forever.

Find an Escape

If you're paying attention at all to anything that I'm telling you and if you're really putting forth some level of effort to make the most of your college experience, then you're going to need some kind of release from the restlessness of college life. My goodness, you're balancing tests and papers and projects and meetings and fund-raisers and parties. It's all so competitive, and it can overwhelm you before you even see it coming. Short of going to therapy, which could end up costing somebody lots of money, you need to find a way to recharge your system.

Just as it is important to meet all kinds of fascinating people while you're in college, it's equally as important to get the hell away from them and to really get in touch with yourself. Time alone in your room doesn't count, and neither does your special private corner in the library. Get off campus. A slice of pizza from your favorite Italian joint in one hand and a good book in the other might do the trick. Or maybe you need to hop in the car and drive the countryside for a couple of hours. Whatever gets your mind back to sane, do it. Find your escape, a place you can go to ease tension and reenergize. College is arguably the most fun, yet challenging, time of your life, and it will pay to get away from it all every once in a while.

Drinks and Drugs

"Chug! Chug! Chug! Chug! Yeaaaaaah! All right! You're the man!" Every corny, stereotypical college movie has the same scenes, and they all involve an array of frat boys and sorority girls and athletes and the math club . . . everybody doing one thing: partying hard. The plot may differ from flick to flick, but the portrayal of college life is always the same, and it always has one constant: alcohol.

Alcohol and other drugs are readily available on college

campuses. Which is sad, of course, but at the same time, you're in college now and the complexities of the social sphere allow you the opportunity to make adult decisions, good or bad. The absence of your parents, along with the ability to acquire illicit substances at your leisure, means that all bets are off. You're on your own to choose which direction your future is headed. (Really. It sounds heavy-duty, and it is.)

Everybody should have fun on the weekends. You've been working hard, you're tense as hell, and you deserve to let loose. But that doesn't mean you have to drink, and it definitely doesn't mean you have to be reckless and immature with your social hours. Now (right now!) is the time to decide how responsible you are going to be when it comes time to make these decisions, which can often be a result of peer pressure. If you delay those decisions until that keg of beer or that joint is right there in front of you, you've already been beat. The pressure will weigh heavy, and you'll cave to chants of, "Puff! Puff! Give!" Discipline yourself now so that you aren't looking back with remorse later.

Once Upon a Drunken Time . . .

Before we get started, I *have* to tell you this story. It's classic, the kind of lore that gets passed from one generation to the next. It was a bitter cold winter Friday evening in New England (are there any other kind of days in New England from October through April?) . . .

A friend of a friend (we'll call him Numb Nuts, because—well, you'll see why in just a minute) goes out for an evening of fun, just like so many of the rest of us did on my college campus. Except he takes it to the next level—and beyond—by drinking way above his limit. I mean, he just keeps at it. He might as well hook up a needle to his arm and start taking it in intravenously. This dude is out of control.

On the way back to the dorm, after making the rounds from one party to the next on campus, Numb Nuts sees this huge pile of snow next to his residence hall. "Who wouldn't want to jump from the roof onto that huge pile of snow?" says Numb Nuts to his friends, who are all thinking—on the inside—"Um, I ain't jumpin' from the roof onto that huge pile of snow, Numb Nuts." Except they call him Travis, because that is his name at the time. Numb Nuts, though, undeterred, somehow finds his way to the roof of that residence hall (two stories high, making this a little over a one-story jump), and exclaims, "Geronimo!" before soaring through the air onto the pile of snow.

The jump isn't that far. And the soft snow should provide for something of a comfortable, cushy landing. But what Numb Nuts doesn't see, in his drunken stupor, is the stick propped out of the pile of snow, the same stick he's destined to land on. And, given his new nickname, I don't think I need to tell you where that stick inserts itself. The good news, if there is any good news, is that given his alcohol intake, he's probably so out of it that he doesn't feel a thing. Now, several (several!) surgeries later, Numb Nuts is one ball short of a double play and he'll be lucky if he has any Numb Nuts, Juniors, running around one day. And it all started with that "one drink too many."

So, now that we know what is possible if we are foolish with our substance intake, let's learn a little bit about how to handle ourselves with poise while drinking, shall we?

Be Responsible

Listen, most people reading this book are going to drink at some point in college. I don't care who you are, how much you love Jesus, or how much He loves you. On some level, even if you just try it once, many of you are going to drink. Which is fine! Shoot, man, it's not that serious. You've still got a shot at heaven.

And some of you are going to take it to the extreme. You're going to measure the amount you drink in days of the week and not times in a month. "I usually take Monday and Tuesday off, go easy on Sunday, and get stupid the rest of the week." Which is not incredibly smart, but hey, it's your life to live.

Most people fall somewhere in between the two extremes and drink in moderation. Truthfully, it's not my concern (or anyone else's), necessarily, although I'm happy to take a page or two to offer some sound "been there, done that" advice on how you can drink responsibly and still optimize your performance outside the party scene. What is my concern, though, and the concern of everyone else around you, is that you show some level of accountability. Drinking yourself into oblivion by yourself in your room is dangerous to your health, but doing the same thing around your peers is dangerous for you and for them. Nobody can control their actions when they are inebriated, so be mature enough to know your limits and stop when you think you could potentially get out of control. Your well-being is at stake, and so are the well-beings of the people you care about. You owe it to them to act with due consideration. Have fun; be wild; be crazy, but don't be senseless.

Beware the Binge

Alcohol is a drug just like anything you might swallow, smoke, snort, or shoot. When abused, it is addictive. It kills off your brain cells, and it can have long-term effects on your organs. Some studies, though, show that alcohol consumption in moderation can have a positive impact on your health, including reduced risk of heart attack or stroke, lower risk of diabetes and Alzheimer's disease, and a potential increase in overall longevity of life. So says Wikipedia.

Twenty-five percent of college students have alcohol-related academic problems. Twenty-five percent! Wow. A staggering statistic. Maybe it's not you or your friend Gertrude, but that number points to what drinking too much can do to one's ability to kick out quality projects and papers, and to one's ability to study for exams. Of all of the distractions that can sweep through and get in the way of your performance, alcohol is the fiercest—because it is just so easy. It's easy to obtain, it's easy to just sit around and knock back a few, it's easy to get hooked, and it's easy to drink over your limit.

Going to a party, having a few beers, and waking up sluggish the next morning with a headache might cost you an hour or so, but it is not incurable. You rehydrate, you take a couple of ibuprofen, and you're back in the game. But getting sloppy drunk (complete with slurred speech, clumsiness, and a sour stomach) means waking up the next day worthless. For the whole day. Or three. Put together two or three binges like that in a month, and you could see yourself slowly slipping into no-man's-land. (Don't make me start telling stories about all the alcohol-related deaths every year on college campuses—from alcohol poisoning to intoxicated slips down the stairs.) Binge drinking—heavy consumption in a short period of time—can keep you from accomplishing what you want to accomplish while you're in college. You can have fun, drink a brew or two, and still enjoy a productive college career, but binge drinking puts you just one more step away from reaching your potential.

Drink Slow

What's the hurry? Seriously. Drinking isn't a race. The first person to finish doesn't get a blue ribbon or the cutest girl in the room. Actually, the opposite is true: the first one to finish their drink usually gets to pass out first, maybe vomits on himself, and gets sent home alone to watch *Nick at Nite* (not that you would be worth a damn *anyway* if sexy Julie was next to you). There is little glamour in being the drunk, so why do it? It probably isn't peer pressure—I know that—because peer pressure in college is much less profound than it was in high school. In high school, if you said, "No, thanks," your popularity could easily be discounted and you were left to hang out with the rest of the goody-goodies. In college, there is most certainly a place for those who don't cave to the demands of the cool kids. And that place is not lonely.

The trick is to sip your drink rather than gulp it. Know what you're drinking (be leery of "Here, try this; I just made it"), and drink it *slow*. If you do choose to drink, it's important to see drinking as a social activity rather than a challenge or a game. You can drink one or two drinks throughout the course of an evening, have fun, and still not have to worry about the unpleasant side effects the next morning. If you're smart and taking it easy, you can go from party to party and drink all night long and still not get stupid wasted. And nobody will judge you either way. (If they do, is that the kind of person you want to surround yourself with in the first place?) In the end, based on what I've seen, slow sippers know how to have a good time, earn respect rather than shady reputations, date beautiful people rather than trashy ones, and wake up in the morning ready to attack their to-do lists. And they also have all their body parts, unlike our boy Numb Nuts, who is still wishing he didn't have those last few drinks that night. It's a win-win-win.

Drink With Somebody Else Around

Drinking alone is not only reaching rock bottom, but it is also slyly dangerous. If you drink alone, it's much easier to tread the line of abuse or dependence without knowing it, and that can be a serious problem. However, having someone around to keep an eye on you offers you the safety net that (hopefully) will keep you in control. No one—from the burliest guys to the tiniest girls—is immune from the dangers of alcohol consumption, and drinking with someone else around is the only way to maintain some level of safety.

Everybody says they won't drive drunk, but the fact is that you don't know what (or who) you're going to do after you've had a few. I've seen some very responsible friends do some ludicrous things under the influence. If you're alone, you might not hesitate to hop in the car while intoxicated, but a friend (hopefully) wouldn't ever let you get behind the wheel drunk.

Just as with academics, you want to surround yourself with a social group that shares your same objectives. If you are hanging around with a bunch of alcoholics, you are more than likely going to drink to their limits and not yours. Which is cool, if you want to waste your life away. Me? I always hung out with Bruno, and since we both had an extremely low tolerance for alcohol, we were able to enjoy our weekends (for the price of a six-pack and few items off the value menu at Wendy's) while also supervising each other's limits.

Successful Students Party Smart

You don't have to drink. Lots of people do (and lots of people don't), but college is plenty of fun without it. My most joyous weekend experiences at Merrimack didn't involve a drop of alcohol. And definitely the most fascinating people I met in college drank very little, if at all. Why? Some people use alcohol as a crutch to live a life they are otherwise incapable of living, and others are perfectly comfortable just being themselves. It's your choice. In the end, though, the most successful students are able to party smart rather than brash.

Now, I know what you're thinking. There's always that one kid who drinks himself into oblivion three nights a week and still succeeds. "So . . . uh . . . what about him?" Yeah, yeah, yeah. And Bill Gates didn't finish college. There's an exception to every rule and regulation, and you're always going to question how Timmy is able to start drinking before noon (in fact, he struggles to function without a couple of beers in his system) and still stay on the hunt for magna cum laude. Well, good for Timmy. He's going places. Based on your own beliefs and your academic productivity, though, are you better off managing your consumption wisely or being reckless with your choice to pound drinks?

The more you drink and party out of control, the more stupid decisions you are going to make. And the less you are going to worry about your academic success. Alcohol consumption and GPAs are inversely proportional: "Eh, I'll study tomorrow." And then you wake up tomorrow with a blistering hangover: "Eh, I'll study tonight." And then nighttime hits, and you're at it again. Rinse and repeat as directed. Once the cycle hits, it is *oh so* difficult to switch gears. The pounding noises in your head give way to the sound of your grades exploding right in front of you. Discipline yourself now to be a solid student, first and foremost. Your social life will follow suit.

A Lecture on Drugs

There are all kinds of drugs available on college campuses, and if you want them, you can probably get them. That ranges from marijuana and painkillers to harder drugs, like ecstasy and cocaine. They're out there, they're accessible, and they're dangerous. In the short term, drugs will fry your brain and take a fierce toll on your physical well-being, and in the long term, we're talking about the collapse of your social, academic, and economic life. And forget about it if authorities catch you with any amount of drugs on your college campus. You're toast, and no amount of praying or pleading will save you. "But . . . but . . . but it's only one joint, and it's not even mine! I was holding it for a friend." It's lit. "He's coming right back." It was in your mouth.

If I have to take the time to school you on the negative effects and consequences of drug use, then you're reading the wrong book. There's no place for drug use in the life of a successful college student, and if you're considering "just hitting the bong once so I can say I did it," you're gambling with your future and taking for granted the many opportunities that you have fought to earn. You'll lose friends, your grades will slip, job opportunities will dry up, you'll go broke (quickly), and there won't be any shoulders left to cry on. Or worse, you could be wheeled away on a gurney because your "clean" drugs were laced or your body has an adverse reaction to your first experience. Any way you toss it, you're talking about the dawn of your demise.

The good news is that *most* people on college campuses are not doing drugs, and you can be among them. Drugs (even tobacco) just aren't cool. As with drinking, form your social group based on the people who have a positive impact on you. If Pierre wants to smoke a doobie (shout out to anybody reading this who grew up in the sixties), you tell him where he can stick his doobie and you go find somebody who's serious about success. Then, sit back and watch the beginning of the end of Pierre. He doesn't have a chance. (It starts with "just one hit," which turns into weekly hits, which spirals into waking and baking, and—well, you get the point. It isn't pretty.)

Get Help for Abuse

If you notice the signs that drinking or drugs are creating a problem in your life or the life of a friend, *get help.* These are issues that can have not only an immediate negative impact but can also extend for many years after graduation. The longer the situation goes, the worse it will become. When you watch or read about all the old drunks who beat their wives, remember that those old drunks were young drunks once. They never got a handle on their issues, they got out of hand, and now their lives are a wreck. Don't think that you're immune (guys and girls alike) to having those very same issues if you start building a foundation of abuse during these four years of college. Simply walking down the aisle with your cap and gown and snatching up your diploma isn't going to solve all those problems from "back when you were young and stupid." Those problems will follow you right off that stage and could plague your professional life.

Signs of abuse can include consuming more than everyone else (or more often); complaining or feeling guilty about drinking; losing control; getting in trouble as a result of substance abuse; neglecting your commitments to work, friends, school, or family; or a consistent change in behavior from the days when you were sober. Or waking up naked covered in Magic Marker. Again. If you recognize any of these indications, it might be time to get your act together and talk to someone. Use the fantastic resources available on your campus!

> There is no shame in getting help. There is shame in knowingly allowing alcohol or drugs to take over your life.

Dating and S-E-X

I had all kinds of sex in college. In all kinds of positions. And in most of the buildings on campus. It was something of a challenge for me. When I was in New York for a weekend, I bought *101 Sexual Positions* for a dollar from some shady-looking guy down at Times Square, and I went back to school and started crossing them off, one position after another, one day after another. I was an animal.

And I did it all with one girl.

There's obviously a very clear reason why I've included the dating section with the drinking section, here in chapter 8: the two are directly correlated. When one goes up, so does the other, which is a shame, but it's yet another reason that you need to act with some level of maturity and alertness when going out. With so many beautiful (and a few funny-looking) people crammed into one place on your college campus, and with beer flowing like water, it can be easy to let go of your inhibition "just this once." Well, "just this once" can turn out to be a big mistake once you see the emotional baggage or sexually transmitted infection that can come along with it.

This first time being away from home can be an opportunity to stretch your wings and discover yourself—on so many levels—and that's how it should be. But that doesn't mean being irresponsible with your sexual adventures. There's a proper way to approach your dating life, just as there is an improper way to approach it. Let's grow and learn, but let's not be reckless and unrestrained.

Take Risks to Find Romantic Interests (Read: Grow Some Huevos)

Let's be honest with each other here. With advancements in social-networking tools, you can be as introverted as a tree and you can look like a toad, and you can still find a girlfriend or boyfriend. My neighbor's cocker spaniel has a Facebook account, and every time I see him, he's hanging out with a new poodle or golden retriever or whatever his chosen flavor of the day happens to be. It really is that easy. So many people are getting to know each other online rather than in person that the need for social skills has been deemed obsolete. Unfortunately, though, in many cases, these people don't even know what to say when they hang out in real life. It's amazing. "So . . . uh . . . that was pretty funny what you wrote on my wall on Facebook." "Ha. Yeah, thanks. I like the pictures you posted." But rarely do those relationships last, because they aren't built on any kind of real-world foundation. Solution? Get to know people in real life.

Now, I'm no Rico Suave when it comes to talking to the

ladies, so I'm not the guy to be giving advice on "spitting game," but I don't think about that when I'm approaching someone. I just do it. I am very open to the possibility that I'm going to get shot down—which has happened *oh so* many times—but that just offers me feedback and makes me stronger for the next one. And the next one. And the next one. It's a character builder, and by now, I have enough character to fill the room you're sitting in. But! I've been dating out of my league since I was sixteen, and I promise you it's not because I'm any cuter than the next dude. In fact, I'm kind of funny looking. My head is *huge,* and my ears stick out of my head like satellite dishes. But I'll talk to a model if she gives me the two-second stare. (The rule is that if someone stares at you for at least two seconds, they're thinking about you, so that's a green light for the approach.)

You just have to do it! If he's wearing a shirt of your favorite team, say something about that. If you're in the same class, drop a line about the homework. If she's reading the same book you are, talk about it. "Ahhhhh, *Harry Potter.* Good choice." Find something—anything—and just go for it. The longer you wait, the more your nerves will build, and you might not ever approach the guy or girl who could be your perfect match. Then, when you finally garner the audacity to do it, somebody else has already approached them and it's too late. Do it! *Right now!* Online dating is for has-beens like me, but when you're in college, force yourself to meet people offline.

Dating Your Friends

Many of the best relationships are built on the backs of the best friendships. While it's true that guys and girls can be nonromantically involved, it's also true that you might start to develop stronger feelings for someone who's been your friend for a long—or a short—time. Great. Talk to them about it. Tell them. "Hey, I know we're just friends, but I think you're pretty much the sexiest person I've ever met in my life, and if I don't tell you this right now, I'm going to carry this baggage forever. So, now you know." I'm serious, man. I'm not kidding. If you plan on walking around with harbored feelings for your friends just because "I don't want to ruin our friendship," then you are in for a sad emotional ride through college.

Listen—you're not going to "ruin" a friendship by going out on a few dates and attempting to take your friendship to another level. That's just plain stupid. I'm good friends with both my ex-girlfriends, one of whom started out as my best friend in high school. I've dated "friends" with whom it didn't work out, and the next day we went about our business as usual. We're talking about maturity here, folks. If you have a healthy friendship in the first place, you'll be able to revert back with no problem. If your friendship is weak, you'll soon find that out anyway.

Even if you approach a friend, proposing the possibility of more, and they say, "Naw, I'm good," that's fine! You tried. You eat your words, and you carry on. It isn't that serious, and it's certainly better than carrying those feelings of, "What if I had just told them?" for the rest of your life. Besides, it might not be a perfect fit now, but now they'll know, and the seed is planted for anything that could possibly happen in the future.

Hooking Up

We can argue this all day long, but in the end, I know I'm right: chivalry in college is dead. Terminated. Lifeless. Deceased. Extinct. Rest in peace, Sir Chivalry. Save Valentine's

Day (a silly, pointless holiday), nobody delivers flowers or goes for walks holding hands like they used to (or so I've seen in old movies). Which is great, because this gives you a distinct advantage, a great opportunity to stand out. We're bringing chivalry back.

What works in your favor is that college culture makes few demands of you in terms of politeness, subtlety, or manners. So, with a little effort, it will be easy for you to exceed expectations and impress upon the lovelies. Also, considering that the two staples of college culture are alcohol and naked time, it's exceedingly important that you are aware of and respect the feelings of your fellow students. (What is it about college that compels everybody to just run around without their clothes on and touch each other? That's a rhetorical question. I don't know the answer. It just is.) Some people are genuinely interested in you, and others picture you without your clothes on while they are talking to you. That's how it is, and you need to be cautious. Be mindful of your surroundings, too. If you choose to run around belligerent at two in the morning, then what kind of crowd do you expect you are going to attract?

Be courteous, people! Be thoughtful. Beyond respect for others, save a little respect for yourself. One in a million solid relationships is built from two people that were carefree and decided to get naked on the first night of meeting each other. If it's going to happen, it will happen when it's right, when it means something. Random hookups—especially those with faulty lines of communication—can easily blur the vision you have for your ideal companionship. Rather than waking up in the morning with regret, how good would it feel to wake up in the morning with a smile on your

> face and the feeling that you might be hanging out with your perfect mate?

More than that, random days should be Valentine's Days in your world. Take flowers just because it's Tuesday, and bring your crush her favorite kind of coffee just because you were thinking about her. (I'm not talking to just the guys here, ladies. Okay, yes, I am.) Don't be a dork about it, and don't be over-the-top, either. Too much gallantry could blow up in your face. Make certain they know how you feel about them, but keep them challenged and wanting more. It's the secret to a healthy, happy relationship. So I've heard.

Have a Life Outside Your Relationship

There isn't a whole lot of elaboration needed here. If you are fortunate enough to find that special someone while you're in college, embrace them; hold on to that person for as long as you possibly can. At the same time, though, work to form a life outside your relationship. Don't cut out the rest of your world—friends, family, school, extracurricular activities—just because you've met the person of your dreams. The worst thing you can do is become so dependent on your relationship that you neglect the life that made you so appealing in the first place. Keep playing soccer, hanging out with Peggy and Sue, and going on rafting trips with the outdoor club. It will be healthier for you, and for your relationship with your significant other. After all, what happens if you put all your stock in your relationship and become so dependent on them for *everything*, and then your girlfriend or boyfriend tells you they don't want to be with you anymore (which will never happen, of course)? You'll scramble to put your life back together while everybody else has already built their social networks.

> Put everything you can into your relationship, but remain independent enough to build a life of your own.

When in Doubt, Keep It in Your Pants

There are three types of people in college: those who run around sleeping with anybody who wants it, those who wait for someone special, and those who are waiting for marriage. You're not going to catch me holding out for marriage, although it's obviously very admirable to wait. Still, for a lot of people—myself included—it means something to disrobe, and there's no shame in that. Some people are looking for a quick romp in the sheets, while others favor an emotional connection and appreciate what it means to look someone in the eyes while they make love to them. Cue the violin.

> If you're not sure what course of action you'd like to take, err on the side of keeping your clothes on. Impulsive fornication will only complicate your life, and if it's meant to be, they will be there tomorrow or the next day. Hold out until you know you're ready. Besides, once you get started hooking up, it just gets easier. "Oh, well, I've already done it, so I might as well do it again." And that's when you can really get yourself into trouble. Hold onto the values that got you this far. You'll be glad you did.

News Travels Fast

The quote on the back of our senior class T-shirts read, MER-RIMACK COLLEGE: WHERE EVERYBODY KNOWS YOUR BUSINESS. It was a cute saying, and it is very telling of the college life-style, whether you attend a large institution or a small one. Especially with the popularity of social-networking sites, news travels so fast that you might not even be the first one to find out you're single. "Hey dude, heard you and Lisa broke up. Sorry to hear about that." *What?* You just have to understand that years ago people had a choice if they wanted to keep their lives private, but today, your business is everybody's business, which is even more reason for you to *make sound decisions.* One misstep can plague you for days, months, or longer—so con-sider the ramifications of your actions before you act on im-pulse. Somebody is going to find out what you did, and they're going to find out fast.

Strap Up

Whether you're ignoring everything I'm talking about (and prepping to shed your clothes with the first cute person you meet) or you're actually learning a thing or two, *drop every-thing and pay attention for one minute.* Maybe I shouldn't have to drop this line of advice, which you've heard since you were thirteen, but it bears repetition for sure, because ev-erybody who is running around with STIs and babies before marriage heard this same advice and didn't pay any attention whatsoever: *strap up!* If you don't have a condom, don't have sex. It's that simple. "But Adam, it's okay. I'm on the pill." *Hell* to the *no!* That isn't going to work, because pills don't protect against STIs. You need a condom. You may not care now, but you will when you start to feel an itch or you haven't had your period for thirty-two days. Don't think for a minute it "will never happen to me." Ha. Every bad-luck situation has been preceded by that remark.

Condoms definitely aren't the ultimate problem solver. You can still contract an STI or find yourself with a little junior to look after in nine months, no matter how many condoms you roll on, so don't think for a second that you're in the clear just because you're "protected." If you make the decision to have sex, understand the risks involved. Get tested *now* for STIs and have your partner tested, as well. One day, when you're married, you can do whatever you want, but right now, even if you're in a committed relationship with the classiest guy or gal in town (who has "never been with anyone except for you"), take the time—and the minor added expense—to put on a condom. You might not be thankful if you do, but you'll be sorry if you don't.

Don't Wait to Get Help

I'm not a psychologist or a health-services professional, so I can't give out advice on how you should feel or act when a crisis strikes, but I do know that you need to get help. Now. If you are raped or sexually assaulted, talk to someone. Please, please, please don't hold that in. The emotional scars from just one traumatic experience can carry forward for a long, long time. No means no. There isn't a gray area here. Even if you've done everything to guard against being abused, it can still happen to you, and it isn't your fault. If you feel that you've been sexually assaulted or raped, go to health services or your counselor or even someone off campus, and talk to them.

If you have any reason to believe you might have contracted an STI, go find out for sure before you run the risk of passing it along to someone else. Many college campuses offer STI testing (and condoms!) for free, so see what services are available to you. It's an even better idea for you to get tested every six months—even if you don't show symptoms—because many STIs remain undetectable and dormant in your body (which doesn't mean you can't pass those along).

You're not being paranoid if you go for help. Waiting too long can have much severer consequences than if you think you've got a problem and nothing comes of it. In this case, there's no such thing as wasted time.

Chapter in Brief

Okey dokey, let's review:

- Meeting people is your responsibility. Not your neighbor's, not your roommate's.
- Meet your RA first.
- Surround yourself with good people, and do everything you can to hang on to those friendships.
- You can drink as much or as little as you want. This is your social life. Remember, though, that successful, happy students party smart.
- Drink slow and in moderation. And never drink alone.
- Don't do drugs.

- Take risks to find romantic interests.
- Hook up when you're ready, but when in doubt, keep it in your pants.
- Wear a condom.
- If you're abusing alcohol or drugs, get help. If you've been sexually abused, get help.

NINE

About Your Health

The freedom of choice in college includes the freedom to eat whatever the heck you want and exercise whenever the heck you want to exercise. How cool is that? Want to eat cheeseburgers with tomato, mayonnaise, cheddar cheese, and bacon for breakfast? Go for it! Meat-lover's pizza as a routine every night at eleven? Make the call! Want to hit the gym for only twenty minutes on Mondays and every other Thursday? Cool! It's your choice.

Obviously, as with the academic, social, and extracurricular activities in your college life, with freedom comes responsibility—the responsibility to take care of your body. Nobody is going to push you one way or the other. It's nice to have a workout partner or someone who enjoys the same foods you do, but really, in the end, the only one who really cares about how you look and how you feel is you.

Look around . . . we are a fat nation. Really. We're friggin' huge. Crummy diets, inconsistent exercise routines, and stress-ridden lives feed unhealthy bodies and minds, which make it even more important for you to establish a healthy program *right now.* The longer you wait, the easier it will be to fall off the edge of no return.

I probably could have wedged the sections of this chapter somewhere else throughout *The Best Four Years,* but they're worthy enough to isolate away from the crowd. Your success in college starts with your physical well-being. And your physical well-being starts now.

Eat Healthy

Of course, I can't be any more clear than to say "eat healthy," but it's easier considered than done—especially when all your friends are ordering food late night and munching on chips and candy throughout the day. Developing your own routine is even more challenging when you have to break away from a crowd. Plus, this isn't drugs or alcohol or promiscuous sex; it's just a little junk food, so it's not that serious, right?

None of this talk about eating healthy means that you have to be a health nut, stuffing veggie wraps, soy burgers (*blegh!*), and egg substitutes down your throat. And you don't have to count calories, either, although it's a noticeable bonus if you do. I'm just saying to be mindful of what you're putting in your body. I love pizza and burgers just as much as the next guy, and I eat them late at night once in a while, but I balance that out by eating healthy, too. There are so many healthy (and delicious!) foods out there that I've always been able to put together a sequence of nutritious meals to go along with the fries and nachos I can't possibly live without. A simple thought to keep in mind is that calories are energy, and if you don't burn them, they get stored away for future use. The more calories you take in, the harder you have to work to get rid of them.

Just as with everything else, it's important to find your own system of eating healthy. Maybe you find that it's a good idea for you to eat super healthy throughout the week and then splurge a little on the weekend. Maybe you're a total health nut and they can't grow broccoli and carrots fast enough for you to consume them. Or maybe you are able to find a nice caloric balance throughout the week. Fantastic. All I'm saying is that if you habitually eat fatty or sugary foods, you're going to blow up. It's that simple.

Snack (Healthy!) Throughout the Day

A wacky routine might actually work to your advantage since you might not have time to stop for all three major meals throughout the day. While you're running around, from classes to meetings to the gym and back to your room, you might not be able to run through the buffet line and sit down with a full plate in the cafeteria. This is where snacking, which you're going to be doing anyway, is an important part of your diet for two main reasons.

First, snacking healthy is good for your energy level. If you're not eating and snacking healthy for any other reason, do it to maximize your energy levels. A candy bar or a sugary cup of coffee might bring you up for a few minutes or half an hour, but then you're going to come crashing down. Conversely, the nutrients in an orange or a granola bar, for example, will keep you going for a longer period of time.

Second, it is actually healthier for you to eat five small meals a day than it is to go hard at breakfast, lunch, and dinner. (Fact. Google it. I'll wait.) Loading up sporadically throughout the day can work against your energy levels and makes it harder for you to work off those extra calories. Trotting around on an empty stomach for four or five or six hours and then filling it up confuses your system and can even make you sick. That said, though, when you do sit down for major meals, you're looking for balance: fruits, veggies, dairy, grains, meat, protein, carbohydrates, vitamins. Find a food pyramid, and mind the serving suggestions. Color your plate with variety rather than a lot of just one thing.

There are a myriad of books out there on cheap and healthy eats that college kids can prepare in no time. Splurge ten dollars for a copy and use it. If health classes are offered on your campus, take one. You'll learn how to prepare a couple chicken breasts or vegetables and rice on the run, and it's a much healthier option than a bag of chips or a candy bar. Besides, when you start preparing your own food, you're talking about saving some serious coin. Cook several servings at once and grub on the leftovers for a few days. That, and start clipping coupons. (Hey, fifty cents can make a difference, buddy.)

If you're smart, you'll start packing trail mix (make your own!) and an apple (or any of about seven billion other healthy snacks) as you run out the door in the morning. Look online or ask one of the staff members at the gym for recommendations of light snacks that are high in protein and low in sugar, caffeine, or saturated fats. When you need that quick boost in between meals, nuts and fruit can keep you going far longer—and with far fewer calories—than what they offer at the campus minimart.

Drink Water

When I started carrying around a bottle of water, rather than drinking soda and tea all day long, I saw a monumental change. Seriously. Read the calories on the back of one can of soda (or worse, add up all that beer you're planning on putting down this weekend), and tally how many extra calories you consume in a week. It's staggering. And when all that water gets too bland and boring for you (by sometime tomorrow), Crystal Light has all kinds of flavored-mix packets to sweeten it up, and they won't erode your teeth like tea and soda will.

Eating Disorders

Eating disorders, like bulimia and anorexia, are prevalent on college campuses and require an immediate response. Your image is not worth risking your health for; and in order to look the way everyone says you're supposed to look, you may be risking experiencing serious health issues. Diet and exercise should be sufficient to achieve a happy self-image, but that doesn't mean that some people won't starve themselves or force themselves to throw up after they eat. If you or someone you know is dealing with an eating disorder, *get help now.* Rarely are these issues solved cold turkey, and often they require the support of friends, family, and trained medical professionals.

But what do I know, right? I just googled "eating disorders" and tried to find the sagest advice I could offer. My friend Laurel, though, who graduated from UNC, has had years of experience battling eating disorders and she has been kind— and forthright—enough to get personal and share her story.

Here's Laurel:

It's all about control. When we feel as though we have no control over life, over grades, over who likes us or who doesn't, we struggle to find something that we can keep the way we want it. Since we cannot control others, we attempt to control ourselves.

Bulimia, anorexia, and all the lesser-known eating disorders (laxatives, spitting, et cetera) are rampant in our society. They seem an easy road to acceptance. The road is much like I-40: just hit it and keep going straight. Right? It will take you to where you want to go and fast. What an illusion! This road is nothing like I-40! This road is more like a Mexican back road. It should have DO NOT ENTER and DANGER signs all along, signs that say turn back now! It's not paved; it's full of holes; it's narrow in parts, and there is a serious chance of falling off the cliffs. And the destination? The destination is far worse than where you began the journey.

It's a drug. It's an addiction. It can kill you—physically, spiritually, and emotionally.

When I was in treatment for bulimia and mild anorexia, I saw the worst of it. I saw airline flight attendants that were so deep into their addictions that they were taking forty-five laxatives a day, ending up with bodies that would no longer function normally. I saw an anorexic woman who had starved herself until her brain shut down, and she died. I saw one woman who, when the food was gone, started exercising nonstop as a way of purging everything she ate. I consider myself blessed to have eventually defeated the worst of my own food issues.

You've heard it said that if you take one step in a negative direction, it will lead to another . . . and another . . . and another. I can attest that it will. So the unhealthy shortcuts you take now might very well lead to years of unhealthy and destruc-

tive food habits. There's a lot of pain and heartache behind that wisdom. Please listen to it.

This is the key—if you are ever tempted to go this route as a means of finding some control over your life, remember this: Bulimia throws off all of the electrolytes in your system and rots your teeth. This is not a pretty sight. Anorexia starves your body's organs (that includes your brain), and you are diminished—not improved—as a result. Eventually, there comes a point of no return. Don't kid yourself. It will not make you more popular. It will not cause you to love yourself more. It will hurt you.

The road to take instead is to discover your true worth and value. If you are eating too much, then find out what is eating you, come to terms with it, forgive whatever you have to forgive, protect yourself in every possible healthy way, look at yourself in the mirror, and say . . . "I love you!" Seriously!

And if you're already a mile down this unfortunate road, then please make sure to seek freedom—whether that help can be found at a counseling service, a health center, or where I did, through a Christian faith-based program. Freedom can be yours!

Exercise Seven Days a Week

That's right. I said it: seven days a week. And that's not just because I was an athlete in college and I *had* to be in the gym seven days a week. For your own good, you need to be active every day of your life.

Now, this doesn't mean you have to hit the cardio or Nautilus machines at the gym every day. When developing your exercise routine, you need balance and variety, or else, A.) you'll get bored from the monotony, and B.) you'll overwork certain body parts and disregard others. Find a formula that allows you to reach your fitness goals. If you want to lose weight, focus on cardio; if you want to gain muscle, focus on lifting; if you want a flat stomach, take an abs class; but don't neglect one in heavy favor of another. Just because you're an animal on the weights doesn't mean your body doesn't need the powerful results that a steady thirty-minute run can provide.

Getting to the gym every day of the week is, for most people, out of the question. Fair enough. Do a hundred push-ups and two hundred sit-ups in your room in between study sessions. Join some friends in the quad to play soccer for a half hour. Go for a thirty-minute walk around campus. You'll clear your mind before returning to other, perhaps more sedentary, tasks, and you can maintain your youthful figure in the bargain.

Then, get to the gym when you can. Maybe you have Monday, Wednesday, and Friday set aside for strength building and Tuesday and Thursday blocked off for cardio. Or the other way around. And then on weekends, you get active somewhere else on campus. The trick is making habit out of your schedule, so that you don't have to force yourself to squeeze in a workout. "No matter what, I'm going to do a half hour of physical activity every day." It should be just as much a part of your daily agenda as brushing your teeth, eating, going to class, and watching your favorite TV show every Tuesday night at nine. Once you see the results of frequent exercise—and everybody else falling victim to the Freshman Fifteen—you'll be all kinds of happy that you are taking the time to care about your physical health.

The best and easiest way to get in the grind of working out regularly is to join a team or find a partner who shares your motivation to work for results. Lifting alone can be monotonous, but lifting with a friend can be fun and, in many cases, more effective.

The Freshman Fifteen

No matter how hard you try, you're still a prime candidate for the Freshman Fifteen. "It's not you, though. It's the atmosphere." Just like the guy you'll read about in the following section, you can be as physically fit as anybody on your college campus when you arrive. The Freshman Fifteen will be a joke to you: "Ah, Johnny, looks like you're about halfway there, kid. Keep eatin'!" Then, as you leave to go home at the end of your freshman year, you notice that you have a flabby stomach and extra skin on your chin, and you wonder how the hell it could have happened to you.

With more fast-food options available every day throughout our country—on campuses and off—and with newer technology that keeps us in our rooms and glued to computer screens, the Freshman Fifteen is giving way to the Freshman Twenty, or worse. It's much, much, much harder now to stay in shape in college, which makes it that much more important for you to mind your physical well-being. *Keep yourself in check.*

A Healthy Life Isn't for Just College

Okay, so forget college for a moment. Think long term. The tendencies you develop now are the tendencies that you will carry forward for the rest of your life. If you develop a way of life that favors a poor diet and limited exercise, then you will continue that lifestyle after graduation (or at least it will be hard for you to break from your normal routine). A mere two pounds gained per year adds up quick. And when it's time for you to come back for a reunion, people will be pointing and exclaiming, "Guess he's still up to his same routine." Even if your metabolism burns food like a furnace now, it will slow down one day, and you don't want to be stuck having taken your health for granted.

Perhaps this is best illustrated by a guy I met a few years ago.

After I graduated from college and wrote *Scratch Beginnings,* I went to work as a skycap at Raleigh-Durham International Airport, checking customers in for their flights. A few days before Christmas, there was a long line and I was checking people in at a fast clip, since we worked for tips rather than a flat hourly fee. As part of the procedure, we had to examine each person's ID to make sure it was, in fact, them and that their ID had not expired. Usually I was pretty negligent about the process, since the TSA officials in the security line were much more meticulous—nothing got by them—but there was one guy whose picture caught my eye. In real life—standing there in front of me—he was in good shape, muscle-bound almost, but in the picture, his face was huge and boasted at least one extra chin, maybe two or three. I paused, looked again at the picture and then back at him. Vaguely, I could tell it was him in the picture, but he had clearly gone through an incredible transformation since whenever that picture had been taken. So I asked him, "What in the hell did you do to lose all of that weight?" He looked at me, grinned, and said that he had gone to the doctor a couple years before. At the time, he was gargantuan, the butt of many jokes, and the first guy to dip out of any social activities that involved—well, walking. The doctor did all kinds of tests, came back in the room, and said, "You are going to die. Seriously. I don't really care either way, because you have done this to yourself, but you are on the path to death. All of your numbers are off the chart, and if you keep up the same lifestyle, you are going to die."

So over the next two years, he was forced to change his life. Or else. He didn't have surgery or take some special pills or go after some crazy healing process. He went on a diet and he exercised, every day. He lost two hundred pounds, and now he looks fantastic.

That's not the point, though. The kicker, as he told me, is that he actually led a pretty active, healthy lifestyle in high school. "But when you go to college, you get bogged down with all these stresses and commitments that you aren't used to, and you start to not care what you eat or when you exercise. You skip a couple days at the gym; you string together a series of unhealthy meals; and then you're in too deep. It becomes habit. Forget the Freshman Fifteen. I did the College One-Fifty."

Of course, most experiences aren't as dramatic as his, but the idea that your previously healthy lifestyle could get tossed to the wind is a very real possibility as you proceed through these next four years. Be mindful of your health, and *don't let yourself go.*

The Way It Can Be

To be honest, though, you might not have to worry at all about this Freshman Fifteen business or letting your physical appearance get out of hand. Sure, some sections of the cafeteria line are loaded with fat, and sure, your time is going to be taken by so many other pursuits, but if you want to keep in shape, you will. And if you don't, you won't. I'm not trying to scare you in this chapter. My experience has more than likely aligned with the people I kept as friends throughout college, since most people I knew were always on top of their physical regimens, if not obsessed with working out. In fact,

I saw a lot of reverse transformations, where plump people I knew came to college, lost all kinds of inches off their waist, and hit the weights hard. In the end, it's a matter of choice, and it has a lot to do with your ability and desire to embrace your new maturity level. Some people grow out, and some people grow up.

A Mental Mess

Even after eating right, exercising every day, and looking great, you still may find yourself mentally or emotionally worn down. The academic and social pressures can weigh on you like nothing you've ever experienced, and they can cause you to have anxiety or even show signs of depression.

It's important that you understand that everyone (everyone!), at some point and on some level, has trouble dealing with the college transition. So, no matter what, you are not in this alone. Most of the more extreme cases, though, sprout from simple stress or difficulties handling new responsibilities and then get out of hand. The name of the game is talking to someone sooner rather than later.

If you notice a general change in your attitude or habits, consider walking over to your college's counseling center to talk to someone. Sometimes a cup of coffee and a venting session with a friend can solve your ailments, but that won't always get it done. Besides, your tuition dollars are paying for the college's counseling center anyway, so take advantage of the free opportunity to smooth out the kinks in your mental armor.

I went to college with what I thought was a very strong mental position. I was away from home on purpose, and I had read all kinds of books about dealing with the move to college, but that didn't prevent me from having three anxiety attacks over four years. Nobody is immune. In fact, overachievers, who are convinced that they are all-powerful, are the most vulnerable. With so much going on at once, anxiety or depression can hit you before you know it and when you are least prepared to handle it—which makes it even more important for you to talk to someone right away.

Chapter in Brief

Okey dokey, let's review:

- Eat right.
- Exercise daily.
- Get help—for you or a friend—at the first sign of trouble.

TEN

Get Connected, Stay Connected

If there's one monumental mistake I saw as I was working my way through my own college years, it was that many of my peers didn't take the time to make—and keep—the right connections. Then, they graduated and thought that jobs were going to somehow magically appear. "Eh, I'll just toss my résumé around to a few companies. I'll get a job. No sweat."

Yeah, okay, "no sweat." A lot of people are living with their parents right now because that's the attitude they've taken. Toss your résumé around? It doesn't work like that, killer. There is a process—from networking to fashioning a pristine résumé and cover letter—and those who follow the process are making major moves in their industries. Sticking out as unique from the rest of the candidates is fine, important even, but that doesn't mean you shouldn't use the process of getting connected while you are still in school. You need to create a foundation for that first day after you walk across that stage to snatch up your diploma.

Do you have any idea how many people go back to school to start another career because they don't love what they are doing? Or they aren't making enough money? In some cases all that may be true, but more often than not, these people were unable to network their way up in their industry. Don't be those people. You've already started to build a future in a career you love, so don't lose traction just because you didn't take the time to shake hands and get cards from the right people.

While You're in School

It all starts right now. From the first day you step foot on campus until the last day you step off, you have the potential to bridge connections that can catapult you to the next level. Or not. It's an attitude. A persona. You never know who's watching or who can make a quick phone call and have you hired on the spot. Seriously. Assistance can come from places you least expect it, but this is about more than simply not burning your bridges. It's about fostering friendships and developing professional relationships that you can use the rest of your life.

Don't be fake about it. You shouldn't be thinking, "Oh, man, I don't want to upset that guy. I might be able to use him one day to get a job." Screw that. You'll drive yourself nuts trying to please everyone. Building a proper network takes time, patience, a smile, and a little elbow grease, but you shouldn't put up a façade in an effort to get ahead. You don't have to. This game is easier than that . . .

Your High School Friends

Before you work on meeting the right people at the college level, take a moment to build a list of people you know from high school—friends and mentors alike—who you'd like to keep in touch with. These don't have to be "best friends forever" or even people whom you correspond with on a regular basis, but these are people whose company you enjoy and appreciate and whom you see heading in the right direction in their futures.

This is one piece of advice that I didn't follow. Which was stupid. All I cared about was playing basketball, and so that's all I did, and in the meantime, everybody I knew from high school was going to Duke or UNC or some dignified New England school to get a top-notch education and then on to fantastic internships and jobs. I'm doing okay, but I could have and should have taken the time to stay in touch with a few choice people.

Your list doesn't have to be long or extensive. In fact, it shouldn't be, since the larger it is, the more difficult it is to maintain. Keep your list of high school connections tight, with only A.) Friends with whom you clicked, and B.) People you see going places. Moreover, work this list outside the bounds of Facebook or Twitter. Facebook is great, but if your professional contacts list is watered down by your collection of 4,672 friends, it will be impossible to control. Ah! That reminds me of a quick piece of advice. When Facebook alerts you that it's somebody's birthday or other special occasion, *send them an e-mail* or some sort of e-greeting. Don't write on their wall. Everybody is writing on their wall, but fewer people are sending them e-mails or greetings, so you'll stick out, for sure, and they'll appreciate that you took the time to do that. A simple gesture that can go a long way.

Start an Address Book

Add to your list from your past, start an address book that you will use to collect the contact information for the valuable connections you are sure to make through college and beyond. Keeping an address book or Rolodex—complete with contact information, what the person does, and how you met them—is important for you to be able to pull up important data for that "one guy I met two years ago who works in the biotech industry, whose name I can't seem to remember." Not only will you be able to quickly refer back to your address book (rather than searching all around for a piece of paper that you misplaced), but you'll also be able to use your address book to . . .

Write Correspondence Once a Week

Keeping in touch is a lost art. Truly. We have become so self-involved that the furthest we're able to reach is an occasional text message or e-mail to say hi. Which is cool, but it's not enough. Let's take it back to the old school.

My Aunt Carolyn is the queen of correspondence. I probably got a card a week from her while I was in college, and each card had an update on life back in North Carolina. Don't misconstrue that as her having time to just sit around and write letters all day long; that lady is a busy woman, always dipping her hand in some volunteer activity or book club or fund-raiser or bridge game. She's active, but she still takes the time to write to those she cares about. And it means a lot. When my mailbox was stuffed with solicitations for every business imaginable, it was refreshing—and it put a smile on my face—to hear from her.

The great thing about correspondence is that it takes ten minutes a week. That's it! You can kick out three cards in ten minutes and be done with it. Think about those who mean something to you, and drop them a line—via snail mail—

every now and then. Maybe include a couple of pictures or a cool magnet that you pick up in the bookstore, or whatever. Among bills and junk mail, they'll appreciate that you took the time to keep in touch. Your parents, your old friends and employers, a teacher or coach or mentor who had an impact on your life—they will *love* getting mail from you.

As your network grows, *stay in the loop*. Keep in touch. You don't have to write cards to everyone every week—that's just silly, and it will look like you're trying too hard—but keep it balanced. If someone does you a favor or made an impact on you, send them a thank-you note immediately, before it becomes a bullet point on your list that you could keep putting off. If you meet someone at a conference or event or meeting on campus and you have a question for them, ask it. If you're interested and they are available, take them out to lunch to probe them on their company or line of work. People love to talk about themselves. If they think you are interested in learning something from them or could use their help, you might be surprised at how available they will be for a free lunch. *But don't be phony with your intentions.* Networking broadens your knowledge and allows you to make more-informed decisions about your own life. And it all starts with correspondence.

Also, go *big* with your correspondence once a year. Everybody sends out Christmas letters and cards with pictures of the family lined up in hideous Christmas sweaters, which is fine, but again, you run the risk of getting lost among everyone else. Sending a mass letter mailing in the summer, for example, keeps your contact list informed of your progress. Then, when the time comes for you to pop the question—"Do you know of any job opportunities?"—you'll be less a nuisance than a fellow graduate who didn't take the time to foster these relationships.

In the end, *one* word-of-mouth reference from your contacts list could be worth more than *fifty* spectacular résumés
sprinkled among the companies in your industry.

Connect With the Career-Services Office

Of course you should maintain a solid rapport with each individual office on campus, but the one that will turn out to be
the most valuable for your post-graduation efforts is the career-
services office. Not only is it a great resource for getting you an
internship, as discussed in chapter 3, but if you play your hand
right, it can help you get your first "grown-up" job.

It's beyond belief some of the jobs I've seen my peers get.
People with embarrassingly low intelligence, who are down-
right unqualified to work in the fields they've chosen, walk
away with their dream jobs, just because of the connections
they've made. How do you think most big-time athletes get
jobs after graduation? Because they went to class? Uh-uh. Most
of them can't tell a noun from bark on a tree or form coherent
sentences when they speak. It's a shame that that's how it works,
but that's not your concern. Instead, this can be your opportunity. Can you imagine if you graduate both well prepared and
well connected to make moves in your field?

Don't discount your career-services office just because you
aren't at Harvard or Stanford. I went to a school you've never
heard of if you live beyond seventeen miles from it—and Jim
Greeley, the big dog in the CS office was connected all over
the country. He had me set up with a list of contacts in New
York City, which is where I wanted to go after graduation—
before I decided to take twenty-five dollars, be homeless, and

write a book instead. Meet the people in the career-services office now, and use them forever. *Your tuition payments are paying their salaries.* If the name of the game is to always be thinking about the next step of your life, the career-services office is your admission ticket.

Attend Networking Events

The most obvious chance you'll have to connect with professionals in your chosen field will be networking events sponsored by your college. These events might host outside speakers; job fairs; business breakfasts, where they invite alumni and executives from area companies to socialize with students; or "speed networking," the speed-dating equivalent of networking, where you'll get two to three minutes to pitch yourself to a prospective employer or pick up any quick advice that you can. Go to these events. Every one of them. And start going your freshman year. You're talking about an hour or so once (maybe twice) a month, and you're talking about *fantastic* opportunities to meet the *right* people. There's a reason your school has invited these guests to come in, so get your butt over to the student center and meet these people. The more your face is seen at these events, the better. Someone is likely to see you once or twice and dismiss you or forget about you altogether. But once they've connected with you three or four times, you're in. For the recruiter, it's just like deciding on what movie to see (or purchasing any other product for that matter): if you hear about a movie once, you brush it off; twice, you think about it; three times, you're going to see that movie. That isn't always the case, of course, but it's a good general rule to go by.

Have Shame

Listen. Networking and establishing connections are not just shake-a-few-hands-and-see-how-many-favors-I-can-get situations. "Yeah yeah. Sounds good, Jack. Say, you wanna offer me that fantastic internship in Chicago this summer?" No, sir. As a matter of fact, it's kind of the opposite. You shouldn't expect anything at all. Think about it: You are a college student. At this time, you have nothing of value to offer. Sorry to slam your ego there, champ, but it's true. You're pretty worthless right now. One day, you're going to be a successful college graduate, at which point you'll have marketable skills to offer, but at this point, you're a nobody. So, when you approach a potential contact or connection, forget altogether how they can help you down the line, or else you'll get caught up being artificial in your approach. (However, *get their info.* It is policy to never offer anyone "above you" your card, but it doesn't hurt to ask for one. They will be impressed, and you will have an addition to your Rolodex.) Appreciate their value to you now—"I'm curious to know what you think about where this particular line of business is headed"—rather than their potential worth to you in the future. Don't sell out your values in hopes to meet the right person at the right time. You'll get nowhere, and you'll look foolish in the process.

Networking is a two-way street—I scratch your back, you scratch mine—and right now you can't do any scratching. Understand and appreciate that you can still make yourself available to network without having a self-serving ulterior motive in mind for later. Besides, savvy business professionals will be able to see through you and will immediately be turned off by your intent to scheme. Learn all you can from everybody you can, work your list, and then revert back to that list when the time is right. Networking may be a tough line to balance, but it's important to do so. Your future depends on it.

Build Your Career "Tool Kit"

Networking is not enough. Actually, it's not even close. Associating with the right people can enhance your expertise and give you an edge on the job hunt, but it's a fraction—a tiny fraction—of your imminent success or failure. The first nine chapters of this book provide suggestions on building your career tool kit. Now, you need to polish it off.

> Starting your freshman year, go to classes or seminars or events that deal with writing résumés and cover letters, learning how to network, or practicing interview techniques. You can learn how to write a résumé or cover letter from an article on the Internet or in a book (or at these events), but use a résumé seminar as an opportunity to pick up extra ideas or have a couple of people look your résumé over. Do you know how many résumés get tossed out just because they are incomplete, appear unprofessional, or are poorly formatted? A neutral-party's eye will catch flaws that you or your parents missed. If a manager sees two hundred résumés at hiring time, you want yours to stick out, and these events can teach you how to do that.

Polishing your networking and interview skills, though, requires real-world application, so don't neglect the power of these (*free!*) opportunities to learn from the experts. You are working with a distinct advantage if you hit the job circuit knowing how to handle yourself one-on-one with the executive or human resources manager. God help you if you graduate cum laude without any networking or interview savvy. You're toast. And even if you already have a job lined up with Daddy's company or you're going to be an entrepreneur out of the gate and you've vowed never to work for someone else in your life, these are still important skills to master.

After Graduation

Yay! You graduated! What a great day. There are hugs to exchange and parties to attend and checks flying at you from relatives whom you haven't seen or heard from since they sent you a check when you graduated from high school. Congratulations. You made it. Now what?

Well, considering that about a billion other people are graduating from college right along with you, your mission is far from complete. In fact, you're just getting started. Even if you have a great job and money saved up and a handsome boyfriend and everything else you need or want, you must continue to develop your career, and the best way to do that is by really kicking your networking into high gear. You need to not only refrain from burning bridges; you need to keep building them. If you've been putting in the work to foster your list of connections over the four years you were in school, then it will be a smooth process for you to transition into networking in the professional world. That said, keeping your network tight (rather than wasting your time chasing potential clients and shaking hands all day long) involves a few key tactics.

Create a Lifelong Affiliation With Your College

Unless you're heavily involved in some Amway or Quixtar scheme, the best networking opportunity you can find—especially at first—is through your college or university. Do everything you can to nurture and advance that relationship. Go to class reunions, join the alumni council, subscribe to alumni publications, and send in announcements when you get married or have a baby or get a promotion. Maintain correspondence. When they offer networking opportunities for current undergraduate students, go. Staying involved with your university keeps open a lot of doors, and it delays the inevitable—that you're going to lose touch with people that you swore were going to be your best friends for life.

Your name is forever attached to your university. When the administration is involved in a scandal, you'll have to hear about it around the office. When your school makes the NCAA tournament for the first time since 1947, you get to gloat all week long. (Until Friday, when they lose in the first round, which is going to happen.) In any event, take pride in your school, and do everything you can to maintain contact with those who have given—and will continue to give—you so much.

Stay in Touch With the Career-Services Office

No, I'm not being redundant here. Just because you graduate and have a job doesn't mean you can cut ties with the career-services office at your college. In fact, it's more important once you graduate.

Even if you had a horrible collegiate experience and you don't ever want to set foot on your college campus again, this is one bridge that you do not want to burn. A *lot* of people who have been unemployed for the last six months are wishing that they had an "in" for another job, but it's very difficult to just call up the director of career services and say, "Hey . . . uh . . . I graduated ten years ago, and I'm just wondering if you've heard of any openings in the IT industry." It generally doesn't work like that. You should already know the director, and you should make it a rule in your life to touch base with them once in a while (once a year!) just to keep them updated on what you're up to. Meet them in college; know them forever. And when a new director comes in, shoot them a note to introduce yourself. This isn't playing the game dirty; this is playing the game smart. Think about it: It is likely that you could change career fields, at which point you will be way up the creek without a paddle, since you've spent your time networking in your own industry. A quick session with a career-services counselor can provide that first "in" that you're looking for.

You put in your time getting an education, and that alone may be good enough to carry you forever. Or maybe you need a leg up once in a while.

Provide Internships for Students

Just as you've been given these opportunities as an undergrad, once you have begun to build an established career, it may be time to think about how your company can recruit students from your college to intern. This is a win-win-win situation. Students win because they get the opportunity to learn and gain valuable experience in their chosen field. Your company wins because they get work done by someone who is energized and motivated to work hard for success. And you win because you look great bringing in talent from your alma mater. Everybody looks good.

Donate to Your School

So, here you are, having put in years of work in school and now in the professional world, and you have built a solid career with a 401(k) and health insurance and all sorts of perks. And a fat paycheck. What are you going to do with all of this money? Buy a house and cars and a home gym, take trips, eat out all the time, pay the neighborhood kid to cut your grass rather than doing it yourself, and *donate money back to your school.*

It's likely—whether you know it or not—that you received financial help from an alumnus who donated money to your college. Think about it: Your tuition paid for the landscaping on your campus and a few people's salaries. That's about it. The lifeblood of the success of a college—public or private— is its endowment. Based on alumni donations, schools can be more aggressive with their advancement into the future, with new buildings and new technology and better professors and on and on. Or not. If they don't receive much in the way of money from their graduates, they won't be able to be cutting edge or progressive, and they certainly won't be able to provide financial assistance to very capable students.

Right out of school, it's going to be difficult for you to spare any change whatsoever. You have debt, your salary is low, you have all kinds of bills coming in, and all you want to do is save up for the down payment on a house. But once you have your feet on the ground and you have extra cash to work with, donate back to the school that helped you get where you are now. They'll love you, of course, but there's a sense of pride that comes with making a difference in the life of someone who is where you once were.

Chapter in Brief

Okey dokey, let's review:

- Making connections and keeping connections is tough work but worth it—if you know how to make the most of them.
- Start an address book and take ten minutes a week to write to your list of contacts.
- Connect with the career-services office now and maintain that relationship forever.
- Once you graduate and are settled in your career, provide internship opportunities for current undergrads.
- Donate back to your college.

Postscript

M y mom cried at my graduation, just as she cried when my brother completed Marine Corps boot camp. I imagine most of her tears were fueled by the fact that I was coming home to crash on her couch indefinitely, but also, she tells me, she was able to see how I had grown over those four years. She was all proud and whatnot, and that made me feel pretty flippin' great. I might have even shed a tear or two myself. After all, I was—and continue to be—dead broke, but I was able to repay my parents in a different way by making things happen on Merrimack's campus.

That said, I'm not the kind of guy to live life with regret, but man, I'll tell you what: there are fifty things I'd do differently if I went to college today, which is the reason I wrote this book. I hope you've enjoyed it, but, more important, I hope you are not dismissing these ideas as the ideas of some has-been who is pointing fingers and saying, "This is what you need to be doing." That's not it at all (although I am most definitely a has-been). I understand that you won't (nay, can't) follow every tip, trick, and tactic that I've written about here, but I hope the book will offer something of a road map as you dive into this exciting stretch of your life. After all, whether you experience success at this first true crossroads of your life is totally up to you and you only—no more hand-holding. How exciting is that?

Take two minutes to call whomever bought this book for you, and thank them. And then go out and make the most of the best four years of your life.

About the Author

————

Adam Shepard is a graduate of Merrimack College, where he majored in business management and Spanish and worked as an RA. He has spent the better part of his years since graduation stringing together a series of words and sentences to form his first two books, *Scratch Beginnings* and *The Best Four Years*. He spends his free time in hotels and on airplanes en route to his next speaking engagement. You can visit his website at ShepardSpeaks.com.

NOTES

BOOKS BY ADAM SHEPARD

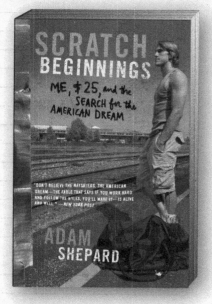

THE BEST FOUR YEARS
How to Survive and Thrive in College (and Life)

ISBN 978-0-06-198392-4 (paperback)

Shepard turns his sights and his charms toward the topic of making the most of your years in college by examining the many aspects (and surprises) of collegiate life, including: transitioning to life away from home, the ins and outs of a tight budget, the benefits of cleanliness, the importance of time off, the subtleties of social life, and much more.

SCRATCH BEGINNINGS
Me, $25, and the Search for the American Dream

ISBN 978-0-06-171427-6 (paperback)

In this spirited and inspiring memoir, Adam Shepard experiments to see if the American Dream is still alive and well. With no concrete plan and nothing but $25 and a backpack, Shepard gets off a train in Charleston, SC, and spends 70 days in a homeless shelter, with the goal of having $2,500, a car, and a place to live by the end of a year.